The Moses Code

ALSO BY JAMES F. TWYMAN

Books

The Art of Spiritual Peacemaking

The Barn Dance

Emissary of Light

Emissary of Love

Giovanni and the Camino of St. Francis

Love, God, and the Art of French Cooking

Messages from Thomas

The Prayer of St. Francis

Praying Peace

The Proof (with Anakha Coman)

The Proposing Tree

The Secret of the Beloved Disciple

Ten Spiritual Lessons I Learned at the Mall

Films

A Chorus in Miracles

Indigo

The Indigo Evolution

Into Me See

The Moses Code

Redwood Highway

Music and Meditations

A Chorus in Miracles

Beloved, I Adore You: Songs from the Anchorhold, Vol. 1

The Best Since Then

The Best So Far

Ecclesia

Emissary of Light

For the Beloved

The Gospel of Jesus

God Has No Religion

Love Is All I Need, Songs from the Anchorhold, Vol. 2

May Peace Prevail on Earth

The Moses Code Frequency Meditation CD

The Order of the Beloved Disciple

12 Prayers

Please visit:
Hay House UK: www.hayhouse.co.uk
Hay House USA: www.hayhouse.com®
Hay House Australia: www.hayhouse.com.au
Hay House India: www.hayhouse.co.in

THE MOST
POWERFUL
MANIFESTATION
TOOL *in the*
HISTORY OF
the WORLD

James F. Twyman

HAY HOUSE

Carlsbad, California • New York City
London • Sydney • New Delhi

Published in the United Kingdom by:
Hay House UK Ltd, The Sixth Floor, Watson House,
54 Baker Street, London W1U 7BU
Tel: +44 (0)20 3927 7290; Fax: +44 (0)20 3927 7291;
www.hayhouse.co.uk

Published in the United States of America by:
Hay House Inc., PO Box 5100, Carlsbad, CA 92018-5100
Tel: (1) 760 431 7695 or (800) 654 5126
Fax: (1) 760 431 6948 or (800) 650 5115; www.hayhouse.com

Published in Australia by:
Hay House Australia Ltd, 18/36 Ralph St, Alexandria NSW 2015
Tel: (61) 2 9669 4299; Fax: (61) 2 9669 4144; www.hayhouse.com.au

Published in India by:
Hay House Publishers India, Muskaan Complex, Plot No.3, B-2,
Vasant Kunj, New Delhi 110 070
Tel: (91) 11 4176 1620; Fax: (91) 11 4176 1630; www.hayhouse.co.in

Editorial supervision: Jill Kramer • *Cover design:* Barbara LeVan Fisher
Interior design: Nick C. Welch

A catalogue record for this book is available from the British Library.

Tradepaper ISBN: 978-1-78817-576-0
E-book ISBN: 978-1-4019-2124-8
Audiobook ISBN: 978-1-4019-6276-0

Printed and bound by CPI Group (UK) Ltd, Croydon, CR0 4YY

To Linda, my first and greatest love.
Although you left this world,
you are forever in our hearts.

CONTENTS

Preface   ix

Introduction   xv

PART I: The Law of Attraction   1

Chapter 1:   A Story for the Ages   5
Chapter 2:   A Gift from God   21
Chapter 3:   Ramses the Great   33
Chapter 4:   A Conversation with God   49
Chapter 5:   Reality vs. Imagination   65
Chapter 6:   The Holy Name of God   75

PART II: The Real Journey Begins   87

Chapter 7:   The Two Paths   93
Chapter 8:   Spiritual vs. Religious   103
Chapter 9:   The Trickle-Down Theory of Enlightenment   117
Chapter 10: Seeing As God Sees   127
Chapter 11: Ego vs. Soul   135
Chapter 12: The Final Step   143

Afterword   153
Appendix
   A Short Course in Manifestation   171
   The 10 Keys to Manifesting Everything You Desire   177
   The 10 Blocks to Manifesting Everything You Desire   193
A Note from the Author   207
The I AM THAT I AM Frequencies, by Jonathan Goldman   209
About the Author   221

PREFACE

Twelve years ago, *The Moses Code* took its first breath in over 3,500 years, changing the world for a second time. Since the book and movie were released in 2008, millions of people have been transformed by the power of the name of God—I AM THAT, I AM. And now, with the release of this updated edition, millions more will experience the same transformative power.

I've often wondered why it took so many centuries for the Code to be rediscovered. Mystics from nearly every spiritual tradition have recognized and tried to communicate this simple, sacred technology, but it is only now that it has been put into a form anyone can master, and once mastered, transform their lives and the entire world.

I remember when I was nearly finished writing the first draft of *The Moses Code*, the subtitle appeared in my mind: *The Most Powerful Manifestation Tool in the History of the World.* The claim gave me pause, but I knew it was perfect. Why? Because it's true, in a very literal sense. I truly believe that this is the answer to manifesting the world we've imagined since the beginning of time. But that never meant that the Code was only for attracting goods into your life—like houses, possessions, or money. In fact, as you'll discover in the pages ahead, that's the *least* of what you'll be able to accomplish. The highest use of the Moses Code is manifesting goodness, not goods, then becoming a source of that same goodness for everyone you meet.

There's a story I've told hundreds of times since this book was released, and I'm surprised I didn't include it in the first edition. It's how I decided to sit down and begin writing *The Moses Code.* It begins with a movie I watched that stirred the imagination of millions of people: *The Secret.* I remember when I watched *The Secret* for the first time, two thoughts ran through my mind:

1. This is a very well-produced movie and is going to touch the lives of many, many people. And . . .

2. This is a very *dangerous* movie, because it tells only the beginning of the story and leaves out the most important part.

The Secret did a very good job of presenting the Law of Attraction, but from a very elementary perspective. What it presented was the "Ego's Law of Attraction," or how to use spiritual principles to get what you don't have, thinking it will make your life better. The focus was on *getting* or attracting *goods*, but the itch it was meant to scratch was left unsatisfied. The "Soul's Law of Attraction" is very different. Its focus is on *giving* rather than *getting* and attracting *goodness* rather than *goods*. To put it simply: the mantra of the ego is "I want," while the mantra of the soul is "I AM."

This is the heart and foundation of the Moses Code: to embrace the I AM Presence that is whole and complete within each one of us.

Here's the second part of the story as it relates to *The Secret.* When *The Moses Code* was being prepared for publication, I decided to produce a documentary that would make the message even more accessible. I worked on the film for a year and was preparing its release when I decided to show it to three friends. After watching it I asked them what they thought, and their answer was not what I expected or hoped for.

"It's okay," they told me. Then one of the men, a well-known director, said that if I was willing to work with him for two weeks, 24 hours a day, he was sure we could turn it into a film that would touch the hearts of millions of people. We were only a month away from the release, and there were already hundreds of theaters and churches ready to screen the film. It was one of the hardest decisions of my life, but I agreed. We worked nonstop, and during that two-week period we reshot over 70 percent of the film, producing a movie that was greater than I ever imagined.

The man who helped me was Drew Heriot, the director of *The Secret.*

Drew seemed to recognize that *The Moses Code* picked up where *The Secret* left off, bringing the Law of Attraction back to the soul and demonstrating a message that the world is ready to hear.

One final piece of information that shows how ready people are to hear and activate this message: a few years after the movie version of *The Moses Code* was released, I was browsing the web and came across something that surprised and shocked me. Several people had uploaded the film onto YouTube in its entirety, breaking copyright laws. At first, I was angry and wondered how I could get it taken down. But then I noticed how many people had watched the film—over *five million.* Instead of having it removed, I contacted one of the people who had uploaded it and asked how I could help. There were millions of people who had never heard of me or the book, yet they were watching and loving the message nonetheless. Who was I to interfere?

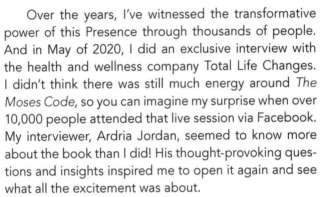

Over the years, I've witnessed the transformative power of this Presence through thousands of people. And in May of 2020, I did an exclusive interview with the health and wellness company Total Life Changes. I didn't think there was still much energy around *The Moses Code*, so you can imagine my surprise when over 10,000 people attended that live session via Facebook. My interviewer, Ardria Jordan, seemed to know more about the book than I did! His thought-provoking questions and insights inspired me to open it again and see what all the excitement was about.

And that's when the flame was reignited.

I felt the fire that launched *The Moses Code* in 2008, which was the same fire Moses experienced over 3,000 years ago when a voice from a burning bush asked him to do the impossible. Maybe you're wondering if it's possible for you to do the same in your life, and the answer is a resolute *yes*. I truly believe that the answer lies in these pages. When you discover the power of the name of God for yourself, nothing will hold you back from achieving spiritual abundance in ways you can't even begin to imagine.

Throughout this edition you'll find new sections, like this one, where I've added new insights and information. I wanted to do more than just rerelease *The Moses Code;* I wanted to make it *come alive* for new and former readers alike. I've also added a bonus exercise at the end of the book to help you embody the information you're about to read.

If this is the first time you're reading this book, I hope you're ready for what's about to happen. You're about to be given the Code for achieving miracles in your life and in the world. It has taken over 3,500 years for this wisdom to come to you, and now that it has, you possess the most powerful manifestation tool in history. Put it into practice, and you'll see for yourself.

INTRODUCTION

It may sound like a grandiose claim, an impressive statement one may write just to sell books or grab attention, but what if it's true? Is it possible that an ancient code exists—a magical formula used by one of the greatest leaders of all time—but has been lost for thousands of years? Interestingly enough, many of us are already familiar with it and have read about the miracles that were realized through its first applications—some of the most amazing events in history. Yet few people are aware of the Code that activated those miraculous occurrences; and when it's applied, it can attract everything our hearts have ever desired.

Why it was hidden and left unused for so long is one of the great mysteries of the ages. However, for the first time, the Moses Code is being shared with everyone, not just a select group of high initiates. In this book, I'll show you how to use the Code to change your life . . . and even the world. The wondrous events recorded in the Bible were a result of this process, and now you can harness its power to create miracles in your own life. You can use it to attract everything you've ever longed for—wealth, the perfect relationship, property, and so on. But the more you experience the Moses Code, the more you'll realize that it's meant for something much greater: to inspire peace and create a world built on compassion and love.

I first became aware of the Moses Code when I was writing *The Art of Spiritual Peacemaking.* Clues and hints rose to the surface as I wrote, almost as if the secrets hidden from sight wanted to breathe fresh air again. Or perhaps humanity was simply ready to see in a way that it wasn't ready to before. When I realized what I was looking at, I knew I had to conduct an experiment to discover for myself whether or not the Code was real.

When I was working on the book, references to the name of God—I AM THAT I AM—repeatedly came up. I sensed the power in the name, but I hadn't yet connected it to the Law of Attraction. It was only as I began studying and applying the name when it became apparent to me: as the subtitle of this book suggests, it really is the most powerful manifestation tool in history.

I'd decided that I would use the Moses Code to help make *The Art of Spiritual Peacemaking* the number one best-selling book in the world on the day it was released. This would require a miracle, and these were ideal conditions for my experiment.

For several months, I applied everything I learned about the Code. When I woke up in the morning, I meditated with it. I even printed a dozen or so copies of the book's cover so that I could practice the exercise throughout the day, pausing for a few seconds and meditating upon my goal whenever I saw a cover posted on the walls in the kitchen, bedroom, and everywhere else in my house. I could feel the energy building, and new ideas were streaming into my mind about how I could realize my vision of it being the best-selling book in the world.

The day finally arrived when my book would be released. I logged on to Amazon.com and looked at its current place. The day before, it was ranked somewhere around 10,000, but early that morning on June 6, 2006, it had reached 300! It seemed that it was on its way up. By noon the book was in the top 20, and at three o'clock it sat at the number 3 position. *Only two more clicks to go,* I thought. By 5 P.M. it was at number two. Almost there.

It sat at the number two position for hours.

It was excruciating. I checked the ranking every hour, but it didn't move. I even rationalized that the title currently in first place was a softcover book, which meant that mine was the best-selling *hardcover* book in the world—but I knew it wasn't enough. When I used the Moses Code, I envisioned it being at the top, and I wasn't going to compromise. It was going to get there; I just had to have faith. . . .

At nine o'clock, I took another look. *Number one!*

I'd like to say that I was surprised, but by then I knew it was real. The Moses Code isn't something I made up or even discovered—in many ways, it discovered me. Recently, there's been so much talk about the Law of Attraction and how we can use it to realize our dreams, which usually means asking, "How can I attract all the things I don't currently possess that will make me happy once I do?" I'm willing to admit that this is an important first step, but I felt that the Moses Code offered something that wasn't immediately present in this formula. In other words, is satisfying the hunger of the ego the real goal, or is there something else within us, something far more significant, that's fulfilled in a very different manner?

The Moses Code is about the next, much more vital, step. How do we satisfy the longing of our soul? The story of my book becoming a number one bestseller on the day it was released is a great example of how we can use the Code to benefit our lives, but is this as far as we're asked to go? Have we been given these sacred tools to simply manipulate reality for our own gain, or are we being called to something higher, a purpose that matches the original intent for the reason why this gift was offered to humanity in the first place?

Although I'll discuss the differences between the longing of the soul and the hunger of the ego later in the book, it may be helpful to say a few words here to prime the pump. The ego is constantly concerned with trying to *get* what it believes it doesn't have, while the soul seeks to give everything it needs, thereby realizing that those things were already present within.

This is the focus of the Moses Code, just as it is the highest goal of the Law of Attraction. The Code was first used to secure the freedom of the Israelites who were enslaved in Egypt. Now it can be used to free *you* from the bondage of your ego. After all, where you live means very little if your mind and soul are oppressed. The purpose of this book is to offer you the most powerful tool in the history of the world for achieving true freedom. What is true freedom, exactly? It's simply the ability to express your Divinity in every situation, in every moment, and realize that you're the creator of the Universe you experience. The ego seeks to enslave while your soul, like Moses, wishes to set you free.

Let me give you one more example of the power contained in this process. I'm writing these words while sitting in a small café near my home in Talent,

Oregon, immersing myself in the ideas and energy of the Moses Code. A few moments ago, I spent some time using the Code to accomplish a particular goal, which was to sell a house I own. I took a few deep breaths, felt the energy of the words I chanted quietly to myself, and then let it go. Even though I spent no more than a few seconds focused in this way, I somehow knew it would have a profound effect.

It is almost 4 P.M. on Saturday, nearly closing time for the café. There are only two other people in the room—a middle-aged couple seated at a table about 15 feet away from me, talking in low voices while looking at a newspaper. I feel the urge to glance over and pay attention to their conversation; apparently, they're from Minnesota and are getting ready to relocate for a job at Southern Oregon University. I notice that they're checking out the real-estate section of the paper and discussing current listings of available houses and townhomes. This is interesting, yes, but it isn't enough for me to lose focus. After all, I'm attempting to write while I'm here. My manuscript is due to my publisher, Hay House, in two days, and there is still some more work to be done.

I turn back to the computer in front of me and type in the words *Moses Code*. The instant they appear on the screen, I feel something tug at my heart: *Tell them about the house you've been wanting to sell*. The house in question is currently being rented, and although I've thought about putting it on the market, I still haven't taken action. Despite this inner urging, I feel like it would be rude to interrupt or even begin a conversation with the couple, since they're so clearly preoccupied. But the feeling is persistent and increases until I finally say hello.

No more than 15 minutes later, we make a deal contingent on them loving the house I have to offer. I know they will, since it is exactly what they are looking for and can be sold for exactly the amount they have in mind. The Moses Code is indeed the most powerful manifestation tool in the history of the world!

Sometimes even *I* need to be reminded.

Twelve years later, as I edited the new edition of *The Moses Code*, I needed to be reminded once again. My house in Portland, Oregon, was up for sale. Though many real-estate markets around the country have cooled during the COVID-19 pandemic, the market in Portland is still strong. I hoped for a quick deal, and during the first week the house was viewed over 40 times—but no offer. The same thing happened the second week, and the third—still no offer. Six weeks later I had to make a decision—take it off the market or drop the price.

My friend Marissa who lives in our Namaste community in Mexico asked me an obvious question: "Have you used the Moses Code?"

I looked at her a bit sheepishly. "No, I haven't," I said. "In fact, the idea hadn't even occurred to me."

"When I was getting ready to sell my house in Santa Barbara to move to Mexico, I was worried because there were no offers for weeks," she said. "Then I did exactly what you suggested in the book. I put notes all over the house that said, 'I AM Happy,' 'A Bidding War Has Started,' and 'My House Sells Above List.' Every time I passed one of those notes, I stopped, took a deep breath, and felt that happiness, then said the words out loud. Three days later, there were multiple offers, and it closed above my asking price. Why do I have to tell you what you wrote in your own book?"

It was a direct challenge. Why hadn't I used "the Most Powerful Manifestation Tool in History" to sell *my* home? I immediately set out and did the breathing technique you'll learn in these pages, and I could feel the energy beginning to move. Something was happening, something wonderful. Suddenly I felt confident that everything was going to be fine.

Two days later, the very day I needed to decide if I would take it off the market, an offer arrived, and the following day another offer. A bidding war had begun. Yes, it's good to be reminded.

PART I

The Law of Attraction

A lot has been said about the Law of Attraction in recent years. People everywhere are beginning to realize that they have the power to attract everything they desire. Actually, it would be more accurate to say that they're starting to understand that they've always had this ability. The Law of Attraction isn't something that we practice some of the time; there's no way to avoid living by this Divine principle.

This book will provide you with an ancient technique that has existed in the world for more than 3,500 years but was hidden away long ago because authorities decided it was too powerful to be arbitrarily wielded. They were probably right. Whether we're spiritually mature enough to do so now remains to be seen, but one thing I'm confident of is that we don't have much of a choice. The world is sitting on a critical precipice, and the decisions we make about how we will or won't implement this wisdom may mean the difference between evolving to the next level of achievement or complete destruction. The choice, it seems, is ours.

This may not be the most important book in history, but I believe that the principles and techniques presented within it are crucial. When the Moses Code was first revealed to the Israelites, some of the greatest miracles in history were performed. Shortly afterward, influential leaders decreed that the inherent energy was simply too vast and potentially dangerous to be used by anyone other than the highest initiates.

Our collective religious history is littered with legends and stories of spiritual masters who evolved to the point where they not only understood the Moses Code but were also able to practice it and achieve extraordinary results. Chief among the practitioners was Jesus of Nazareth. It's now time for all of us to master the Code as well—not just to add riches to our lives, but to create a world based upon the laws of compassion and peace. If we continue to use this remarkable tool simply for our own gain, then we'll be lost.

This may sound ominous, and that is, indeed, the intention. You're being offered the most powerful tool in history for creating your reality. This isn't a New Age fairy tale; it's real and true. We need enlightened souls to finally manifest the world of our dreams. It's easy to look at the earth and see the devastation of unconscious manifestation. Our planet didn't arrive at the brink of such terror on its own but through our collective decisions. The question now is simply: Will we choose this again, or will we finally and resolutely decide to follow the call of the soul rather than the pandering of the ego? Whatever we genuinely feel, the world and everything in it will transform in order to match that belief.

You have an essential and individual role to play, and that's why this book has found you.

Part I of *The Moses Code* discusses the story of Moses and the basic spiritual makeup of the Code. Then the tone changes dramatically, emphasizing once again the importance of your choice to create and consciously evolve.

For now, relax and enjoy . . . you're about to go on a journey that will change your life!

Most of us were taught to relate to the Divinity of Jesus rather than his humanity. And yet Jesus himself said that anyone who believes in him would do even greater things (John 14:12). A question I often ask people is, "Who said those words? Was it Jesus the man, or was it something much greater?" It was actually both—Jesus, who was a person no different than you, as well as the fully realized I AM Presence that's within you as well. When Jesus says, "I AM the Way, the Truth, and the Life" (John 14:6), he was speaking from a fully realized soul perspective, not the limited personality or ego perspective. In other words, he was speaking as the Christ. This book is meant to bring you to the exact same experience—to speak and to live from your own I AM or Christ Reality. It may seem like an impossible leap right now, but as you go further in this book, you'll discover it's the simplest thing in the Universe.

CHAPTER ONE

A STORY
FOR THE AGES

You've probably heard the story of Moses leading the Israelites out of Egypt, an astounding accomplishment that began with him standing before a burning bush, listening to the voice of God. But have we ever really heard the deeper message being communicated, not only to Moses but to each one of us? Is it possible that a code is hidden within this story—a secret that gives us the ability to attract everything we desire into our lives? Could this be the most powerful gift God has ever bestowed upon the world?

An actual Code that God imprinted in the message shared with Moses is now being shared with you. This is the real Secret! It was hidden from humanity for good reason—because it's literally the most powerful force in the Universe—not just the words, but the activation of the Code itself. Don't take this lightly. I do my best to approach it with great respect because I know that it's

5

the very lesson that can change the world and lead us to the experience we've all been seeking.

Did Moses receive this cryptic message from God, and did God intend for us to also uncover the key to realizing all our dreams, easily and automatically, drawing into our lives everything we've ever asked for?

If so, is it possible for you to use this same secret today and for the rest of your life, achieving what the rest of the world would call *miraculous*?

Welcome to the Moses Code!

Let's begin by revisiting the story, setting the context for us to finally comprehend the most spectacular secret ever concealed from humanity.

We're told that Moses was born an Israelite slave in Egypt, but due to either profound luck or Divine Intervention, he was raised a prince among his oppressors. According to a law set forth by the Pharaoh, every male child born to Israelite slaves was to be drowned in the Nile. Jochebed, the wife of Amram, a Levite, gave birth to a son and kept him hidden for three months. However, when she realized that he'd soon be discovered and killed, she set her infant son adrift on the Nile in a small craft made from bulrushes coated in pitch. A short distance down the river, the Pharaoh's daughter found the baby and adopted him as her son. She named him *Moses,* meaning "to draw out."

Here's an interesting side note to our story: Moses's sister, Miriam, watched the boat as it floated along the Nile toward the city, then to the royal palace. When she saw the Pharaoh's daughter rescue the child, Miriam approached her and asked if she'd like an Israelite woman to nurse the infant. She suggested Jochebed—Moses's real mother—and she raised him to be the adopted grandson of the Pharaoh. From the beginning, Moses had his feet in two separate worlds . . . and had two distinct mothers with very different dreams.

The story continues when Moses is a man, a brave leader of the Egyptian empire. But one day, something happens that forever changes his life. Moses is among the slaves when he sees an Egyptian soldier mistreating an Israelite man. Outraged at this abuse, Moses kills the soldier and hides the body in the sand, hoping no one will ever discover his crime; however, he soon learns that his secret has spread throughout the ranks of the slaves. Fearing that his grandfather, the Pharaoh, will be informed of his deed and have him put to death, Moses escapes to the Sinai Peninsula and finds refuge with Jethro, a priest from Midian. Moses ultimately marries Jethro's daughter Zipporah, and he stays with them for 40 years.

Now we've arrived at the pivotal moment when the great mystery of creation was revealed to humanity, only to be hidden away upon the first demonstration of its enormous power. It was one of the very first conversations with God, a conversation that changed the world. The time has finally come for each one of us to experience and embrace it.

One day as he was leading his flock up Mount Horeb, Moses saw a bush that burned with a bright fire, yet the fire didn't consume it. He turned to look at the marvelous sight, and God spoke to him.

What did God say to Moses?

These words have been shared and loved by billions of people throughout the world for almost 3,500 years. Did anyone realize that this was one of the greatest gifts God had ever given to humanity? Very soon you'll be among the first to understand the Moses Code and apply this amazing technique in your own life, but only if you choose to embrace it yourself.

Let's examine some of the passages from the book of Exodus that describe this conversation with God. It begins by saying:

> God called to him from the bush and said,
> "*Moses, Moses.*" And Moses said,
> "Here I Am." (Ex 3:4)

Pay close attention to Moses's reaction upon hearing God's voice streaming from the fiery bush. He doesn't run away in fear. He also doesn't fall to the ground, saying, "Why are you speaking to me? Don't you know I'm not worthy of this?" Instead, Moses turns toward the bush and says, "Here I am." This may seem like an innocuous response, but if we look a little deeper, we realize that it's far more significant. However, it's impossible to understand the impact of his statement until we continue a little further in our conversation.

How willing are you to say what Moses said when he heard God's voice? Are you willing to say, "Here I am" just as he did? I promise that God is speaking to you right now, not through a burning bush but in many, many other ways. God speaks to you when you're reading a book and you come across a sentence or even a few words that spark a feeling or an impulse within you, reminding you that you are whole and complete. God speaks to you when you're in someone's company and they say something that triggers the light inside you. You know what I mean, because we've all had that experience. We all know what it feels like when the Holy Spirit "tickles" our soul. The question is—are you willing to say, "Here I am," or run away in fear?

Hearing Moses's response, it's almost as if God is pleased. God then says to him:

> Do not draw away. Take your shoes from
> your feet, for the place where you
> stand is holy ground. (Ex 3:5)

Why is this place holy? The obvious answer is because it's the spot where God has become manifest and known in the world. God's presence is being experienced through an ordinary bush on a mountainous ridge. And the fact that this very same bush is burning with a fire that doesn't consume it is certainly miraculous. It makes this ordinary moment quite extraordinary.

It is significant that God comes to Moses through fire. Jesus once said, "I have come to set the world on fire, and how I wish it was already burning" (Luke 12:49). Fire is transformative and cleansing. Is it possible that we're welcoming a new fire into the world, one that will transform and cleanse the whole planet? This is why, in my opinion, the Moses Code is gaining such renewed prominence—because the *time has come*! You wouldn't be reading this book right now if you weren't feeling the heat of this fire. The only question is, Will you follow Moses's example and use it to change the world?

But is there another possibility for why this ground is so holy?

God clearly understands God. This is something we can all agree upon, since God is omnipotent and omnipresent. Therefore, if God knows itself to be in all places at all times, would the Creator single out one place above all others as holy just because God's presence is being experienced there by one particular man? Is it not the will of God to be seen and felt in all places and in each person? From God's perspective, all places are holy because God is everywhere. This means that the Creator is unlikely to identify one physical location as more blessed than another. We may do this, but God wouldn't, because it would be the same as limiting what's limitless.

The greatest difficulty of our humanness is that we're unable to view or experience God in all places at all times—our minds simply can't conceive anything so vast. But does the Divine also share this limitation? If so, then God would be as restricted as we are, unable to know itself as *Itself.*

Is it possible that when God asked Moses to take off his shoes, God was speaking much more intimately than we first guessed? Moses said to God, "Here I Am." It's almost as if God smiles at him and says, "Ah, well said, Moses; indeed, here *I Am*. This ground is holy because it's the spot where you have known yourself to be who you are."

You may be thinking: *Wait a minute! Are you saying that God was pleased because Moses seemed to recognize himself as one with his Creator?*

The answer is *yes!*

For thousands of years, we've been sold a lie, and this has led to the suppression and dismissal of the Moses Code throughout the world. We've been told that we're weak and vulnerable, unable to do little more than eke out a meager existence on Earth. If we're lucky, we're able to accumulate a relative degree of comfort, maybe even own a few houses and build a big bank account, but none of that will really ever satisfy us. Our purpose is to live and then die, hopefully with a few moments of joy in between. We've imagined ourselves in a prison from which we can never escape, and we've convinced ourselves that this is our real home.

But what if the door to that prison cell was never locked? What if the world we live in is nothing more than a projection of our thoughts about ourselves, and God has never shared that vision at all? If God is all-powerful, all-knowing, and fully present in every moment, is it possible that the Creator would rejoice when we realize the truth?

Hold on before you answer. Your response will determine your entire experience of life and how willing you are to accept everything that God intends for you. Your answer will determine how open you are to receiving miracles, and ultimately, cracking the Moses Code.

Read those last few sentences again, because they're so important and hold a very important key for unlocking the Code. You've been told a terrible lie that you willingly believed—that you are vulnerable, weak, and out of control. I promise you that God does not see you in this way at all. In God's eyes, you are invulnerable, invincible, and controlled by the power of grace itself. Yes, you are one with God. Maybe you can take a deep breath and say those words: "I AM One with God." Say them over and over until you feel the spark of recognition. It's like prying open a door; once the door has been cracked open, the light begins streaming through and you're able to see what has always been there. And it's the same for you. The light is beginning to stream into your mind, and as it does, everything comes into perfect focus.

Let's continue with the conversation between Moses and God. God says to him:

> I am come down to deliver them [Israelites] out
> of the hand of the Egyptians, and to bring them
> out of that land unto a good land ... flowing
> with milk and honey. (Ex 3:8)

God is making a great promise to Moses: granting the Israelites a passage out of Egypt and into a new home where they'll be abundant and free to live as they please. Once again, let's look to the nature of God and decide if the rest of us are included in this promise. If God is in all places at all times, then this could be more than a historical decree that was made to one particular individual or group to the exclusion of the rest. Is it possible that God's vow is made to every person who listens, meaning it's being made to you right now? If you're willing to listen and believe, then you'll discover, just as Moses did, that God never breaks a promise to anyone. If this is true, you're being led to the same land flowing with milk and honey—in other words, the place where your dreams become reality.

God is telling Moses that he'll lead the Israelites out of bondage into the promised land. In this place, we're told, Moses and his followers will have everything they need, and nothing will be denied them.

Why? Because they are the chosen children of the Creator, worthy of all goodness and blessings. Most generations believed that this was a gift reserved for specific people (the Israelites). And according to this belief, God favors one group over another and is therefore willing to offer the "chosen ones" something that the rest can't receive.

But is this really true? God says, "I am come down to deliver them out of the hand of the Egyptians and into the land of the Canaanites, and the Hittites, and the Amorites, and the Perizzites, and the Hivites, and the Jebusites" (Ex 3:8). In other words, there are lots of other groups already there. Perhaps these people never left the promised land, or they were able to use the Code to arrive there earlier. All we know for sure is that God's will is for them to be free, and this can't be reserved for a single group of individuals. Freedom is meant for everyone, as is the land overflowing with abundance.

In the end, Moses is really no different from any of us. Faced with such an extraordinary gift, most would fall into the ego pattern that has ruled our lives for so long: fear.

Your ego, otherwise known as *the part of you that perceives itself to be separate from God and everything else,* believes that you don't deserve anything, especially not the fulfillment of your greatest dreams. A

15

well-known acronym for the ego is Edging God Out. How can we edge out the Creative Force of the entire Universe and still have what our soul most longs for? The ego forces us to fall backward and *play it safe* and never comprehend the infinite potential that lies within. Like Moses, we say to God:

> Who am I, that I should go unto Pharaoh,
> and that I should bring the children
> of Israel out of Egypt? (Ex 3:11)

God may have replied, "Who are you *not* to bring them out?" We usually wait for someone else to get the job done, never realizing that there really is no one else. God is choosing you in this moment to receive everything you desire. When you do so, you'll be a living example of the great secret that will make you rich beyond your wildest imagination.

And remember, we're not just talking about being rich in the worldly sense. Yes, that is part of it, but only a small part. What we're really focusing on is richness, not just riches. As Jesus said, "What do you benefit if you gain the whole world but lose your own soul?" (Mt 16:26). You are about to receive richness beyond your wildest imagination, which is actually what you've been most afraid of. I know that sounds a bit silly. Why would you be afraid of achieving wild richness in your life? The answer is simple: because there's still a very big part of you that believes you're not worthy or that you don't deserve such a gift. Don't worry about that for the moment, though. It's good to notice this ancient feeling and fear, but as we go further you'll see that there is a way to help it dissolve on its own.

And now we come to the critical question and answer that the entire Moses Code is based upon. God has given Moses a task, one that seems impossible. In fact, God even tells Moses that the Pharaoh will never listen to him or consider honoring his demand, which doesn't seem to surprise Moses. After all, the Israelites were responsible for building half of Egypt. Without their forced labor, the Pharaoh wouldn't be able to construct his vast temples or modern cities. In short, without Moses's people the Pharaoh would be lost, and he wouldn't take this loss lightly. Moses needed something more—something to tell the Pharaoh and his own people—that would convince them that this was the will of the One God.

> And Moses said unto God, "When I come unto
> the children of Israel and say to them, 'the God
> of your fathers has sent me to you' and they say
> to me, 'What is his name?' What shall
> I say to them?" (Ex 3:13)

A name has great power. It not only identifies people and separates them from others, but in many cultures, it defines who they are—that is, a name bears the essence of the individual. When Moses asks what name to give his people so that they may believe he's telling the truth, it's a very big request. It must be a name that incites passion and dedication; it also must be worthy of the Creator of all things, the single Source of life in the entire Universe. What kind of name can encompass the power and majesty of such a being, as well as contain the magic and mystery that God deserves?

> And God said to Moses, "I AM THAT I AM.
> This is what you will say to the children of
> Israel: I AM has sent me to you." (Ex 3:14)

I AM has sent him? Remember that this is what Moses said to God when he was first called to the burning bush: "Here I am," or in some translations, "Here am I." Whether or not Moses realized it, he'd identified the power of God with his own, and God was pleased. In fact, when Moses shared this name with the Israelites and then the Pharaoh, miracles began to take place all around them. One after another, the world began to conform to the idea that Moses held in his mind: the Israelites should be freed from Egypt. In the end the force of this demand, backed by the name of God, was undeniable, and the Pharaoh had no choice but to concede. God's children were allowed to leave and seek the promised land where all their dreams would come true.

How can we harness the power of the name of God in the same way Moses did? Calling someone by their actual name indicates intimacy. If you called me Mr. Twyman and I said, "Please, call me Jimmy," it would mean we're on a first-name basis. It means that I want to be close to you, and that I want you to be close to me. Think about that from the perspective of Moses's conversation with God. God is saying, "This is who I AM. Call me that. And if you do, great miracles will follow." Is it possible that you're being told the same thing? Is it time for you to be on a first-name basis with God?

But here's the question we now need to answer: Having witnessed the supreme power given to them by God through this name, why did the Israelites hide it away, rarely to be used again? For centuries and even millennia, many people have believed that humans should never utter the name given to Moses. It was unspeakable, and so the magic contained within it was concealed from the world . . .

Until now! You're going to learn how to unlock the Moses Code; in doing so, you'll attain everything you've ever desired. Do you believe this is possible? Will you be like Moses and ask for more proof?

If it's evidence you need, I'm all too ready to give it to you.

CHAPTER TWO

A GIFT
FROM GOD

Are you ready to have the same conversation with God that Moses enjoyed? I assure you that it's the key to receiving everything in the world that you're entitled to. You thought you deserved lack, sickness, and ultimately, death. Why else would you be experiencing these things if you didn't want them?

This may be the hardest concept you'll ever have to admit: the idea that you've created everything in your life, including what doesn't serve you well.

Once you do accept it, though, you'll also be able to accept happiness, abundance, and perfect balance. That's why you're here! It's the reason why you opened this book . . . nothing else will satisfy you now.

———✦———

It's true—taking full responsibility for everything in your life takes great courage, but I assure you that it's the first step toward putting the Code into practice. You are a victim only of your thinking. Change your thoughts about your world, and your world will change on its own. You've probably heard this before expressed in different ways, but have you ever put it into practice? Keep reading and you'll learn how.

It's time to throw open the steel door that has kept you apart from your heart's desire. The Moses Code is about to be unlocked, but I'd be remiss if I didn't provide you with the following warning: *once you open this door, it can never be shut.* You'll know too much once you've been exposed to this secret, and you'll never be able to fall back into ignorance again. From this moment on, you'll realize that you have the key to everything you could ever dream of. If you choose not to use this gift, then it will be no one's decision but your own.

Also be aware that this tool you're about to be given is far more powerful than your mind can possibly comprehend. The words may seem simple, but they unlock a source of energy that created everything you perceive. Literally! You were created by God, and therefore you possess all the qualities of God, just as you possess the genetic information of your earthly parents and ancestors. A scientist can explore a person's DNA and determine who his or her children are—and this same idea applies to God. You're about to explore a code that's been locked inside your soul; and in doing so, you'll discover that you're the child of the Divine, possessing the same power to create as God.

MONOTHEISM VS. POLYTHEISM

When Moses asked for God's name, he was given what may at first seem like a cryptic statement. It wasn't a normal name God offered but an assertion indicating a *presence,* transcending ordinary definitions. God said, "I AM THAT I AM," then commanded Moses to tell the people that "I AM has sent me to you." This seems to solve the argument of the day: Are there many gods, as the Egyptians believed, or only one God, which was the foundation of the Hebrew faith?

This wasn't the first time such ideas were presented in Egypt. From around 1353 to 1336 B.C., the Pharaoh Akhenaton, who rejected the old gods and initiated a monotheistic worship of the sun god Aton, ruled the country. Since Moses is usually regarded to have lived no earlier than 1300 B.C., it's clear that the Egyptians had already endured at least one attempt to institute a society built upon the belief in one supreme being.

The statement, or name, "I AM THAT I AM" tells the Hebrews and Egyptians that God does indeed exist, and there's viable power in saying the name. Moses has apparently been given more influence than even Abraham, the father of three great monotheistic religions, because he's aware of God's name, while Abraham wasn't. In the sixth chapter of the book of Exodus, God tells Moses that Abraham was never given the name even though the Creator appeared to him. With this name, Moses confronts the most powerful ruler in the world and compels him to release every Hebrew slave in Egypt. What was it that finally compelled the Pharaoh to commit such an unlikely act?

Miracles!

By using the name of God, Moses is able to:

- Turn his walking stick into a serpent

- Transform the Nile into a river of blood

- Create plagues of frogs, lice, flies, locusts, and other terrible things

- Kill the firstborn of every Egyptian

- Part the Red Sea and destroy the pursuing Egyptian army

This is more than enough evidence to create a strong impression on anyone. In the end, Moses and the Hebrews were left alone to follow their destiny: finding the promised land.

And now you'll use the name of God just as Moses did in order to realize your greatest dreams. The process you're about to learn will align your power with the Power of God, giving you the authority to draw into your life anything you desire. *Authority*—that's the key, for without proper authority, the cosmic and elemental energies lie dormant before you. However, when the name and authority of Divinity enliven them, they spring forward and hearken to your command, as they recognize you as God's co-conspirator.

It's important to realize that Moses was feeling many of the same emotions you might be feeling right now. Perhaps you're thinking, *Who am I to perform miracles in my life and in the world?* When God told Moses to go to the Pharaoh and demand the release of his people, Moses responded in a very human way. But God's answer was revolutionary: "I appeared to Abraham, to Isaac, and to Jacob, as God Almighty; but by my name I was not known to them" (Ex 6:3); God is saying, "Now that you know my actual name, you have something none of the others had. Miracles will spring from your willingness to access then activate my name in your life—the I AM Presence that's within you right now. Get ready, because you're about to be shown how to do just that."

Exercise #1:
The First Form

What do you want to attract in your life? This is your first step. You may choose to start off with something small or go after your heart's desire. It's totally up to you, since the Moses Code doesn't recognize levels of difficulty. It treats everything the same—as extensions of God and, therefore, something that you deserve. You're also an extension of God, so it's logical that you're entitled to whatever you request. This may seem like a distant leap for your mind, but with continued practice you'll know it's true.

Have you chosen to focus on financial abundance, a particular object, or the perfect relationship? Write it down on a piece of paper, and keep it in front of you so you can clearly see your goal. Now go to a place where you can relax and be alone. At first you'll only practice this exercise for a few moments, but after a while it will become a habit, and you'll find yourself using it throughout the day. Once you're alone and relaxed, take a deep breath.

With your eyes open, look at the sheet of paper in front of you and say out loud: "I AM THAT." Exhale as you recite these words, and then as you inhale, continue by saying, "I AM." The sound will be different because you're reciting the second phrase on the in breath. Repeat this circular breathing and speaking as you stare at what you've written down. It's important to feel the emotion of "already having" what it is that you're asking for. I'll explain this more in a moment. For now, create the emotional feeling that you've achieved your goal, continue to breathe, and repeat the chant.

Let me explain what you're actually doing. When you breathe out, saying "I AM THAT," you're claiming that you're one with the desired state or object. You're affirming that you aren't separate from the thing you're asking for; rather, you're contained within it and it's contained in you. In other words, you're expanding the definition of who you are and drawing into your being something that you believe you deserve.

This claim—that you're one with the thing you desire—is actually a statement of truth. In fact, you aren't separate from anything; you're an aspect of the all-pervading life of God. You're one with God, so you're one with all things that are also one with God. Does this make sense?

Perhaps not to your logical mind, but your soul understands this statement all too well, and that's why the Moses Code works. It's as if you're finally acting upon the knowingness of your soul instead of your mind, which is at best confused about everything it perceives. It sees everything as separate and alone, whereas your soul views everything as intimately connected to its source.

When you inhale, saying "I AM," imagine that this is God's response to you, claiming and accepting the thing you desire to draw into your life. You say to God: "I AM THAT," and God answers: "I AM." The name of God now comes full circle and easily draws the thing you're focused on into your life.

Pay close attention to this next part of the explanation. If you can understand it, even with the limitations of our limited minds, you'll realize the power of using the name of God to manifest your desires. When you say, "I AM THAT," to God, God doesn't answer you, saying, "You are." The Creator replies, "I AM." In other words, God is saying through you: "If you claim it, then I claim it, too, for we are *one*!" "I AM THAT I AM" now becomes a single statement rather than two. It is God speaking to God, and God answering God. And what would God give itself? *Everything!*

Now you understand the beginning level—the first form of the Moses Code. As you practice it and experience the results, you'll have direct knowledge of the power of God's name, just as Moses and the Israelites did. The miracles that will naturally occur in your life will reflect the greatest ones that humanity has ever known. Will they be as distinguished as the parting of the Red Sea? Of course, because to God, a small miracle is equal to one that changes the world. They're no different, because eternity isn't concerned with concepts such as big or little—only the mind is interested in that, and the Moses Code leads you away from the mind and into your *soul*.

I said earlier that it's important for you to *feel* as if the thing you're asking for is already yours. This is one of the most vital aspects of the Moses Code. God will always give you exactly what you want in life. Unfortunately, we often ask for the things we don't want, and they're given to us because that's what we're really asking for. In other words, if you feel that something isn't yours or that something is beyond your reach, you won't receive it—your heart's desire remains outside your grasp. Your feelings are the key to drawing what you wish for into your life. Divine Energy flows in the direction that you design. If you *feel* that you don't have something, then it is the *not having* that the energy responds to. If you feel that you *already have* the thing that you're asking for, then God responds accordingly.

Your feelings steer the wheel that guides the ship of your life into the port of your highest desire, setting the course your destiny follows to the fulfillment of your dreams.

Exercise #2:
Attracting What You Want

Make a list of some of the things you'd like to attract into your life. Now scan the list and pick the one that really stirs your spirit. What gets you most excited? Which of these inspires you and calls upon you to practice the Moses Code? This will be your first attempt at using this sacred technique, so when you're ready, find a quiet place where you can be alone. Relax and make yourself comfortable.

Imagine that you're sitting in a movie theater watching a film of your life. You're viewing a scene sometime in the future when you've already attracted the thing you chose from your list. Visualize it in as much detail as you can. Are there others there with you? What are they saying? Listen to the conversations, and pay attention to the smallest details. Make it as realistic as possible.

Now take a deep breath and imagine that you've actually jumped into the scene. You're no longer watching it but are now living it, connecting to all the emotions. If you're wanting to attract the perfect relationship, visualize that you're with your soul mate and feel the love and gratitude appropriate to the moment. Get involved in the scene. With all your energy, feel the emotions of *having*.

As you continue to experience the scene, begin practicing the Moses Code. While exhaling, say aloud, "I AM THAT," believing that you've actually become the goal you seek. Now take a deep breath in while saying "I AM," knowing that God has claimed it through you and as you. Hold on to the vision, letting the chant add energy and momentum. Allow the feeling of *having* swell within you, completely filling your heart.

When you feel that you're done, take a deep breath and keep your eyes closed. Permit the energy to sink into your soul as you relax. Most important, give gratitude for having successfully attracted the thing you've set your heart on. Notice that I wrote this as if it has *already* happened. This is what you must do as well—pull the energy of the future into the present moment.

You've done everything you need to do. Your energy and appreciation are the only ingredients you needed to supply. Now that they've come together, the Moses Code is complete within you.

CHAPTER THREE

RAMSES THE GREAT

How was Moses, elderly and altogether forgotten, able to stand before the most powerful man in the world and compel him to free the Israelites from bondage? Is there a difference between the worldly force wielded by the Pharaoh and the Divine Energy that Moses was able to generate by using the name of God?

Let's remember that Moses—a formerly well-respected member of the royal family in Egypt—was forced into exile and had been tending sheep for 40 years. If he was around 20 years old when he was banished, he would have been 60 by the time his encounter with the burning bush took place. That doesn't seem very old from our perspective, but in the time of Moses, reaching that age was almost unheard of. The average life span of a male was approximately 40 to 45 years. Taking that into consideration, Moses would have been around 90 by today's standards—clearly not possessing a great deal of worldly acumen or influence.

On the other hand, the Pharaoh enjoyed all the power of the known world. It's hard to imagine what it would have been like to rule a country like Egypt at this time, but suffice it to say that his dominance is legendary. Many of the most innovative architectural achievements in history are attributed to this era, and the Pharaoh Ramses was the king of kings.

Let's take a deeper look at this significant character in this drama. . . .

Ramses II (or Ramses the Great) is often regarded as Egypt's greatest ruler. He was responsible for constructing some of the most elaborate cities and temples in the region, as well as leading his army to spectacular victories, establishing the Egyptian empire as the most powerful force on Earth. He was born around 1279 B.C. and is believed to have taken the throne sometime in his early 20s, ruling from 1279 to 1213 B.C., a total of 66 years and two months. Some claim that he lived 99 years, but it's more likely that he died around the age of 90 or 91. This would mean that Ramses knew Moses personally when he still lived among the royal family, although it's unclear if he was aware of Moses's Israelite roots.

Ramses the Great accomplished many things in his life; more than 3,000 years later, he's regarded as one of the most prolific rulers of all time. His focus before the battle of Kadesh (the war that ultimately secured his command) was building temples, monuments, and cities. He constructed the city of Pi Ramesse in the Nile Delta as his new capital and main base for the Hittite war. The city, which was established to honor his eminence, was situated on the remains of Avaris, the capital of the Hyksos. This is also where the Temple of Set was located. Pi Ramesse was a sacred city for Ramses because it's where he supposedly harnessed the energy of the deities Set, Horus, Ra, Amun; and of his father, Seti.

In other words, Ramses was imbued with the power of the gods, a quality that surely aroused the interest and contempt of the Israelites with their monotheistic religion. But regardless of these disputes, the king had ascended to a godlike stature and was the very essence of authority and might.

It's easy to imagine what Ramses must have thought when Moses first entered his lavish and stately palace. Did he recognize him—perhaps a distant memory from his own childhood? Did he remember Moses's fall from grace and flight to safety, never to be heard from again . . . at least until that moment? All we know for sure is that Ramses wasn't at all impressed, for it was clear who was in command. Moses undoubtedly arrived in the garments of a wandering shepherd, while Ramses was attired like a god. Moses may have stood for the Israelites, but they were slaves whose sole importance lay in their strong backs. The Pharaoh represented everything that was civilized and good in the world—the embodiment of worldly stature and power. Moses, it seemed, didn't stand a chance against him.

But that isn't how things turned out!

Moses was most likely as unsure of himself as Ramses was confident. As the shepherd entered the room to face the Pharaoh, he probably wondered not only if his people's dream of freedom was about to end, but if his own life was about to be extinguished as well. His initial escape from Egypt secured his continued existence, but now after many decades, he'd been commissioned by God to return and face a different kind of music. The Pharaoh's majesty would have made Moses's chosen simplicity seem naïve and unsophisticated, which wouldn't have fared him well.

But there's another possibility to this scenario. The fact that Moses finally did decide to follow through on God's request may have signified that he was certain of his ultimate victory. God told him that using the Sacred Name would give him authority and power, and it seems that Moses was convinced. Is it possible that Moses had experimented with the Code before making the journey? If he'd done so and witnessed for himself the creative force inherent in God's name, then he'd have stood before Ramses empowered and confident.

How would the Pharaoh have reacted to such self-assurance? The fact that Moses wasn't immediately punished or killed illustrates that Ramses chose to entertain him at least for a little while. His command eclipsed Moses to such a degree that he might have been somewhat curious. Ramses would reserve the right to change his decision, putting Moses and the Israelites back in their place as soon as his curiosity wore thin, which is, in fact, exactly what happened.

Moses began by asking Ramses to grant the Israelites a reprieve from their work, allowing them to go into the desert for three days to make sacrifices to God. Ramses was apparently astounded by the request and did the opposite. Until then the Egyptians had been providing the Israelites with enough straw to make the bricks for construction. Ramses—in order to show Moses who was really in charge—forced them to gather their own straw, thereby doubling their work.

But Moses kept coming back, insisting that God's wishes be fulfilled. It was now time to prove once and for all that the Pharaoh's reign and the will of God were on a collision course . . . and the king would surely lose.

If this were a Western, this would be the point where the showdown takes place. Moses had been practicing his manifestation techniques, learning how to turn his staff into a snake and turn water into blood, as well as other strange and phenomenal demonstrations of power. But this was *happening* at a time when magic and magicians were a great resource, especially for a ruler of Ramses's stature. When he was finally in front of the Pharaoh, Moses threw down his staff and it began writhing upon the ground. The Pharaoh's magician performed the same transformation, but Moses had the upper hand. The snake representing God's emissary ate the Pharaoh's snake, and the contest was on.

Although Ramses's magicians were able to duplicate some of the miracles Moses manifested, it's clear that they weren't winning the competition. A series of plagues then descended upon Egypt, apparently at the behest of Moses using the power of God's name.

As recorded in the book of Exodus, the miraculous occurrences included the following:

- Rivers and other water sources were turned to blood (7:14–25)

- Frogs (7:26–8:15)

- Lice (8:16–19)
- Either flies, wild animals, or beetles (8:20–32)
- Disease on livestock (9:1–7)
- Unhealing boils (9:8–12)
- Hail mixed with fire (9:13–35)
- Locusts (10:1–20)
- Darkness (10:21–29)

Little by little Ramses realized that he was up against a power he didn't understand. At one point, he even agreed to let the Hebrews have their three days of sacrifice, but only if Moses reversed the plague of frogs. When all the frogs suddenly died, leaving behind a terrible stench throughout the region, the Pharaoh became so angry he rescinded his promise. This ultimately led to the most terrible plague of all: the firstborn child of each Egyptian family suddenly and inexplicably died.

As we expose this final blow to the Pharaoh's evaporating position, an important question needs to be answered. After all, the God presented here and in most books of the Old Testament is very different from the God described by Jesus and many other great prophets. In this story, Moses has been given the vast energy inherent in the name of God, and it's used to wreak havoc upon the Egyptian population, even including murder.

THE GOD OF THE OLD TESTAMENT

We may do well to ask ourselves if the story we've been passing down—the biblical account of Moses and the Israelites' ultimate victory—is completely accurate, or if it has been conveniently embellished over the last 3,000 years in order to back up the claim that the Israelites are the chosen people of God. The God we're presented with in the book of Exodus is jealous and vindictive, quick to react when the chosen emissary is ignored. This doesn't reflect the more modern version of God as an unconditionally loving deity. In many ways, I've been mixing these two accounts in this book, portraying a benevolent, compassionate God while still relying upon a decidedly more ancient concept of a supreme being who desires obedience at any cost.

So which of these depictions is true?

It's impossible for us to know for sure how much of Moses's story is factual. Scholars and theologians have struggled with this question for years, and since I claim to hold neither of those titles, it might be best to leave this for others to debate. What we're concerned with here is something more significant: Regardless of whether the story is completely accurate, *what can it teach us about ourselves today?*

In many ways, things haven't changed much since Moses and Ramses had their showdown. Religions war against other religions in an attempt to prove their "rightness" before God and man. I personally believe that the Code is being revealed at this time because we're finally ready to accept the great responsibility that comes with it. While I'm writing these lines, the world is experiencing great uncertainty. The pandemic of 2020 is out of control in many parts of the world, and entire countries are falling by the wayside. My own country—the U.S.—has never experienced so much division and chaotic government in its history. But as the saying goes—it's always darkest before dawn. I believe *The Moses Code* is enjoying this resurgence because we're ready to say *yes* to what our souls are longing for, not just to our lower impulses. We're finally able to lay aside the judgmental, vindictive God of history and embrace the compassionate, loving God that has always been here, waiting for us to open our spiritual eyes.

The lesson, in my opinion, is to realize our oneness with the Divine, which was accomplished (at least for a while) by Moses and the Israelites through the use of the Holy Name. We're just beginning to understand that this name contains mysteries that have eluded us until recently. (After the Appendix, I've included an article written by the sound healer Jonathan Goldman, which reveals a startling discovery regarding the mathematical and vibratory properties of the name of God.) These mysteries indicate that there was a powerful intention behind the Holy Name and even how the story of Moses was presented.

Most people are also aware that the first five books of the Hebrew Bible, the Torah, seem to contain messages and prophecies that weren't uncovered until complex computer programs were used to break the codes. *The Bible Code,* a book by Michael Drosnin, became an international sensation when it revealed that text in the Torah prophesied the assassination of Israeli prime minister Yitzhak Rabin. Apparently, Rabin was told not to attend the ill-fated event in question, but when he decided to ignore the warning, it cost him his life.

An even earlier seeker of hidden messages in the Bible was Isaac Newton, who believed that the Bible is a "cryptogram set by the Almighty . . . the riddle of the Godhead, the riddle of past and future events divinely fore-ordained. . . . This prophecy is called the Revelation, with respect to the Scripture of Truth, which Daniel was commanded to shut up and seal, till the time of the end. . . . Until that time comes, the Lamb is opening the seals."

Suffice it to say that the mysteries of the Torah are vast, so it's no wonder we're still discovering the enigmas contained within it. But why has the Moses Code been so overlooked?

The book of Exodus, the second book of the Torah, describes the method in which the Israelites were released from Egypt and ultimately led to the promised land. This feat was achieved by creating miracles stimulated by Moses using the name: I AM THAT I AM, or in Hebrew, EHYEH ASHER EHYEH. The fact that most Orthodox Jews chose to put away the Sacred Name or speak it only in the temple meant that its true function was forgotten and the original pronunciation was lost.

In the meantime, two other religions—Christianity and Islam—were born from the original root of Abraham, but by then the name had already receded from attention, at least as it was originally intended.

But there was one person who didn't forget . . .

Jesus!

In the Gospel of John 8:58, Jesus says, ". . . before Abraham was, I AM."

By using the words *I Am,* Jesus declares that he is one with God, made evident in the next verse by the scribes' and Pharisees' reaction: "Then took they up stones to cast at him."

Jesus didn't simply say the Name—he claimed it. To the scribes and Pharisees, this was the ultimate blasphemy, for their vision of God was unapproachable and beyond human connection. When Jesus came along and basically said, "I AM God," they responded in the harshest manner.

And yet, this is the essence of the Moses Code— the realization that we're all one with God, and once realized, to act with the power and passion of God in the world. When Jesus did this, miracles followed him everywhere he went. He was the embodiment of the name of God, even to the point of conquering death.

From our perspective, this is the ultimate and highest objective of the Moses Code: to realize our eternal nature and transcend death in a similar fashion. Jesus said:

> Truly, truly, I say to you, he who believes in me,
> the works that I do shall he do also; and greater
> works than these shall he do. (John 14:12)

If this is true, then the ability to perform miracles sleeps inside each one of us. *A Course in Miracles,* a modern spiritual text, says that miraculous occurrences are natural and indicate an alignment between God and our own consciousness. It also states that there's no order of difficulty in miracles. For example, creating a parking space in an overcrowded parking lot operates according to the same laws as raising another person from the dead. Alignment with our Source—otherwise known as God—is the key, and when this is achieved, anything is possible.

Calling upon the name of God joins us with the source of power that enables us to create miracles. It acts as a bridge between this world and Heaven, drawing into our lives everything we need to be happy and completely fulfilled.

Today, we live in a world where we're safe from being stoned to death for harnessing this Divine Energy; in fact, there's no reason for us to hold back any longer! Thousands of years have passed since the world received this gift, but it's needed more now than it has ever been before.

Exercise #3:
Overcoming Limitations

When Moses stood before the Pharaoh, he was confident in the role given to him by God, but because of a debilitating speech impediment, he was unable to speak to Ramses without the help of a friend.

Like Moses, we all have similar obstacles that rob us of our self-confidence. Perhaps you've experienced a difficult childhood or have some form of physical limitation.

Begin by writing down a list of the factors that may be blocking you from achieving your heart's desire. Leave a space after each of these for the next part of the exercise.

Once you've listed the limitations in your life, let's balance them with the Moses Code, turning them over to God to be used just as God used Moses. Go back and read each of the things on your list, and then take a deep breath. Ask yourself, *How may God use this to bring love into the world?* For example, if you wrote, "My parents are both alcoholics," on the next line write: "This experience gives me compassion to deal with others with addictive behavior." Now break the sentence down to one word that amplifies the positive intention. In our example, it would be *compassion:* having parents suffering from alcoholism has given you the compassion you need to help others. Choose one or two of these words as you go through your list, and write them on a separate sheet of paper so that they can be easily seen.

Now we'll turn back to the Moses Code. While looking at one of the words you wrote down—one that reflects the gift you've received from your so-called *limitation*—begin the chant. If your word is *compassion,* breathe out saying "I AM THAT," as you feel your heart filling with empathy and loving-kindness. Then inhale, saying "I AM," knowing that God has claimed this quality with you and as you. Stay in this awareness and continue the chant until you feel enlivened by this new mind-set, realizing that just as Moses used the Code to uncover his gift and overcome his limitations, so can you draw upon this gift whenever you need it.

CHAPTER FOUR

A
CONVERSATION
WITH GOD

One of my greatest mentors and dearest friends over the last 20-plus years has been author and scientist Gregg Braden. When we first met in 1998, the two of us, along with Doreen Virtue, decided to embark upon a Great Experiment to see if a large group of dedicated individuals could impact world events through the use of an affirmation-based form of prayer.

We set a simple goal: choose a specific place in the world where cooperation and compassion seemed present anywhere but there and project the *feeling* that "peace prevails now." We've conducted this experiment in Iraq, Israel, and many other locations; and we're convinced that this type of prayer is not only a powerful force, but perhaps *the most powerful force in the Universe.*

Here's an example of one such experiment. In 1999, the U.S. and its allies were on the brink of war with Iraq. Saddam Hussein had forced the United Nations inspectors out of the country, and there didn't seem to be any way to avoid an international conflict. Gregg, Doreen, and I were speaking at a conference in Florida on November 13 and we decided to announce a worldwide meditation, praying peace into that tenuous and dangerous situation.

E-mails were sent through many online communities, and by the time the moment of the vigil arrived, hundreds of thousands of people from around the world were joining us. We were onstage together, leading the prayer, which was being broadcast over the Internet, and we could feel the energy. I remember thinking that it was "raining" peace, but it wasn't until the next morning that we realized just how powerful the effect had been in Iraq.

According to the morning news, President Clinton had decided to begin the bombing campaign the evening we were engaged in prayer; in fact, fighter jets had been deployed and were waiting for their final orders. But precious time passed as the pilots wondered about the delay. Then, to the astonishment of everyone involved, Clinton ordered the jets back to their ships. Some moments later, as if reconsidering the command, the jets were sent back into position. Once again, the "go-ahead" to drop the bombs never came, and the jets returned with their weapons cache still filled. A stand-down order had been given, but no one really knew why.

Does it amaze you to know that this happened at the same time as hundreds of thousands of people were focusing on peace for that region? Hopefully it doesn't surprise you at all, for that would mean you already accept the power found within this secret tool for manifesting anything you desire, including peace. What we were able to do on an international level, you can accomplish in your own life.

I could share many stories like the one above, proving the energy and power that can be generated by practicing the Code. In each case we were asking people to generate the feeling that the prayer was already accomplished—the same as you're being asked to do when you embrace the name of God: I AM THAT, I AM. In other words, you're not asking to be made into something you are not, but acknowledging what and who you are, this and every moment. I remember several years ago when I stood on a hill looking into a village held by ISIS in Syria. Around 100 of us were there while a terrible battle raged beneath us. We could actually hear the guns and see the tanks rolling through the town. At the same time there were millions of people around the world ready to generate the feeling of "I AM Peace, I AM," then project it into the village below. The moment arrived, and everyone on the hill sat down to begin the meditation. Then a silence suddenly fell across the whole landscape below us. The guns and the tanks stopped as if the soldiers and the fighters could feel the impact of our prayer. We all held still and continued to extend the prayer "I AM Peace, I AM" until the 15-minute meditation was over. Then another interesting thing happened: the instant the meditation ended, a pack of wild wolves began to howl a short distance below us. They couldn't have been more than 200 feet away from where we sat, and after a single minute, they stopped—a signal, in my mind, that our prayers had been heard.

AN IMPOSSIBLE MISSION

Imagine being Moses, an old sheepherder whose glory days had long since passed, when God asks him to go to the most powerful man on Earth and ask for the release of most of his workforce. The word *impossible* seems too small here, yet Moses hardly hesitated. He immediately began the journey to the Pharaoh and made his demand, knowing all too well the response he'd receive. But he wasn't dismayed, for he knew he held a secret that the Pharaoh could never understand—a secret that had more strength than an entire army. It took a short while for the Pharaoh to be convinced, but when he realized that neither he nor his own magicians could match the power Moses wielded, he opened the doors and let the Israelites leave Egypt.

Now you possess the same secret as Moses—the Sacred Name of God. When you learn how to unleash its amazing energy in your own life, you'll discover what the greatest minds in history understood: *the power of God is within you, and you can do whatever you want with it.* You've actually been using it all along, just without your conscious recognition. Now that you're aware, you can use it to create goodness for yourself and everyone around you.

In his book *The God Code,* Gregg Braden puts forth the premise that God's name is literally encoded into every human body. According to Gregg's research, the basic elements of DNA—hydrogen, nitrogen, oxygen, and carbon—directly translate into specific letters of the Hebrew alphabet (YHVG), which then translate into another one of the original names of God. He believes that when we realize the signature of God is carried within the cells of every person on Earth, humankind will have the evidence it needs to overcome evil with good. In short, we'll be able to achieve the greatest desire of every human—*peace.*

"Beyond Christian, Jew, Muslim, Hindu, Buddhist, Shinto, Native, Aboriginal, white, black, red, or yellow; man, woman, or child, the message reminds us that we are human. As humans, we share the same ancestors and exist as the children of the same Creator. In the moments that we doubt this one immutable truth, we need look no further than the cells of our body to be reminded. This is the power of the message within our cells."

— GREGG BRADEN

The Moses Code is in our bodies and our minds. Every cell sings the same song, the song of creation, and every heart beats to the rhythm of that melody. It's an energy that transcends anything our minds can comprehend and unites us with elemental forces that evade the intellect. The most learned scholars on Earth will never be able to dissect the complexity of this secret, yet the most innocent among us resonate with it already. It is who we are, and when we unlock the Code, we're really unlocking the deepest part of our own nature.

I really like thinking about the name of God—I AM THAT, I AM—as a song or a melody that every cell in your body responds to and resonates with. As you practice the Code more and more, you'll feel your body begin to react in a positive way. Perhaps you'll feel a beautiful vibration or a subtle shift—just as you might when you hear a piece of music that touches your heart. Follow that energy. When you sense its approach, take a deep breath and see where it takes you.

So how do we tap into the Moses Code within us?

If the name of God is within our very DNA, it stands to reason that it's the actual foundation of our lives. God's name, then, creates a resonance pattern that when activated aligns us with anything we desire—no matter how large or small. As I mentioned earlier, *A Course in Miracles* says that there's no degree of difficulty in creating miracles. In other words, a big miracle is no more difficult to create than a small one because they operate according to the same laws. Once we understand these laws and apply them, wondrous happenings will naturally occur on their own.

This means that there's no limit to what you can achieve! It doesn't matter how much abundance you envision, how happy you want to be, what kind of car you want to drive, what style of house you want to live in, or what type of relationship you want to enjoy—if you understand and apply the secret found within the Moses Code, attaining all your goals will be no harder than manifesting $20.

In essence, unlocking the Code means entering into the same conversation with God as Moses did. The fact is that we're engaged in this dialogue every moment of our lives. We sometimes call this prayer, but for most of us, our concept of praying is very limited. In reality, however, every thought is a prayer that creates a magnetic attraction, pulling whatever we're thinking about into our lives.

Unfortunately, we tend to think of prayer as asking for something we want based on what we think we need or don't already have. If we pray and don't receive what we want, then our prayers of petition sometimes turn into prayers of coercion.

The Red Bike

There was once a young boy who heard about using prayer to attain what he wished for. His parents told him that if he asked Jesus for what he wanted with enough conviction, then Jesus would surely give it to him. That night, the boy knelt down at the side of his bed to pray.

"Dear Jesus, I really want a new red bike. My mother told me that if I pray hard enough, you'll give it to me. Please give me a new bike."

The next morning he woke up to find there was no bike. That night, he knelt down again to pray.

"Dear Jesus, I really want that new bike, and I believe that you'll give it to me if I pray hard enough. Please give me a new bike!"

The next morning, once again, there was no bike waiting for him.

The boy was making final preparations for school when he passed the mantel where a statue of the Blessed Mother was resting. He found a piece of rope, took the statue from the mantel, and wrapped the rope around it. Then he put it in his backpack. When he arrived at school, he opened his locker, placed the statue inside, and locked the door.

That night before getting into bed, the boy knelt down to pray once more.

"Dear Jesus, if you ever want to see your mother again . . ."

The point is that the moment petition no longer works, we immediately turn to coercion: if I can't talk God into giving me what I want, maybe I can force the issue.

The Moses Code doesn't work when you ask for what you want, but rather, when you *feel* and *know* that you already have the thing you're seeking. Then the very thing that you're seeking is automatically drawn to you because the Universe doesn't understand lack. It knows only abundance because God only gives, or expands.

Even though the task God was asking Moses to complete seemed impossible from any rational frame of reference, Moses confidently went forward and changed the world. When we enter into the same conversation with God with the confidence that everything we ask for is given to us, then we will do the same. The issue isn't whether or not it's being offered; rather, it's whether we're able to open wide enough for it to be received.

The problem is that our conversations with God are usually one-sided, not because God doesn't answer us but because we usually don't listen to the answer. God answers by giving us what we ask for. It's that simple.

Jesus said: "Ask and you shall receive." Do you think those are just nice words that he didn't really mean? What if Jesus meant every word? What if it's a law that works every time, whether or not you're conscious of it?

Think about it for a moment. God gives you everything you ask for every time. That can be a pretty scary thought if you're surrounded by what you think you *don't* want. Guess what? There's no such thing as not wanting what's in your life. I wish there was a way to soften that terrible blow, but there's really no way around it. The sooner you realize that fact, the better, because then you'll start taking full responsibility for everything you experience—not just the things you like.

This is such an important point I want to add a bit more to make sure you understand. Everything that's in your life right now, every experience you encounter, is there because you literally "prayed" it into existence using the Code. That's a hard pill to take because we don't want to admit that we want things that hurt us, or seem to cause conflict or separation. You might be asking why you would ever want to welcome anything that causes you pain. The answer is simple, though difficult to accept: because you think you deserve it! There's something in each one of us that believes we deserve pain, or that we don't deserve the fulfillment of our Soul's Desire. To go a bit deeper, your ego, or that part of you that wants to remain unfulfilled, actually strives to keep you from realizing what you're reading right now. It wants to keep everything on the outside rather than realizing that everything rises from within. This is not meant to cause you greater pain, but to inspire you to acknowledge how much control you actually have over everything in your life.

If you go around believing that you've asked for some things to happen but not for others, you'll never be able to break the Moses Code. You'll be sentenced to a prison of your own design, sitting behind a door that isn't even locked. Touch it and it swings open, but only when you consider the possibility that you have the power of God within you every moment of your life. You built the prison, you condemned yourself to it, you threw yourself into a cell, and you closed the door. There's only one problem:

God didn't give you the power to lock it!

Let's stop for a moment and give thanks. This is good news, for it means there's a built-in default system completely beyond your control. There's a part of you—a very big part—that doesn't want to hear what I just wrote. In fact, it will do anything it can to avoid it, even at the cost of your own happiness. When the ego is forced to pick between happiness and victimhood, it will always choose being a victim.

This is one of the strangest ironies of your ego's life, in that it doesn't have your best interests at heart. Your ego would rather see you suffer than accept the truth. Why? Because the truth requires you to become responsible for everything that happens to you. Ah! This is too much to embrace.

It would prove that everything you've ever experienced—both good and bad—has occurred because you wanted it to. It means you aren't the weak little body your ego wants to believe in. It means . . .

Houston, we have a problem!

It would mean that you have the power of God within you, and there's nothing beyond your control. As I've said before, this is something to give thanks for, because now you have the wisdom and ability to make a new choice, one that reflects your freedom instead of your bondage. When you make choices from freedom, the result is more freedom. Once you accept that, you can receive everything you desire by simply recognizing that you already have everything you want . . . and then more of what you wish for will be drawn to you.

> *Once you learn the Moses Code and practice it,*
> *your abundance will reflect your freedom,*
> *and everything you've ever desired will be yours.*

Everything in your life is there because you called it into existence. In other words, it's impossible for you not to use the Law of Attraction simply because you've always possessed the creative power of God within you—it isn't something you can begin to practice but something you've always done. You create as God creates, drawing into your

61

life all the things you focus on and love. If there are things in your life you don't want or that don't serve your highest good, the question isn't why are they there, but why do you love them so? Do they represent something you haven't yet discovered? Perhaps they're the limiting beliefs or concepts you hold that would prefer to control your life rather than release it. If this is true, then the question becomes: Do you want to continue fueling them, attracting more and more evidence of your insufficiency, or is it time to finally release them into the light?

Why do we love our inadequacies? The response will vary from person to person, but the simple answer is that our deficiencies prove the belief that lives right behind them—that we are unworthy of receiving the gifts God intends for us. We don't deserve love, happiness, and peace; instead, it's more likely that we deserve separation, sickness, and death. This is what the ego would have you believe, but your soul, which is always aligned with God's will, has a very different idea.

God's will for you is perfect joy. However, you can't enjoy this until you share his will, for without your consent, God would be working against you rather than with you. Until now, most of us have said, "I don't deserve anything so blessed." Is this true? Have your past deeds really blocked God's love, which has the power to flow past these errors? If they have, then we all have a very big problem, because to one degree or another, we're the same.

Fortunately for us, they haven't.

It's time to realign your vision of yourself with the vision of God, who sees you as perfect and whole regardless of what you've done in the past. God's love is unconditional, and there's nothing you can do to interrupt it. Accept this and love will flow into your life; continue to hold on to the ego's illusions and love will be blocked, even though it's certainly still present.

Exercise #4:
God's Will for You

On a blank sheet of paper, make two columns: one for your beliefs and one for God's. In the first column, write down a list of some of the beliefs or experiences you've manifested in your life. Perhaps you're not consistently happy, you continue to live a life of sacrifice and lack, you think you're not lovable, or you believe you don't deserve to be loved. God wants you to be happy every moment of your life and abundant in every way. Therefore, you've been trying to contradict God's will, and in doing so, a struggle has ensued.

It's time for you to finally admit that you've lost this struggle.

If you have to do battle with anyone, let it be with God, because it's a fight you'll always lose. You don't want to win the ego's war, for it leads nowhere except to your continued unhappiness. When you surrender to the Divine within you, all the blocks to the gifts of God are removed and his love will naturally flow toward you.

Now, in the second column, write down God's answer next to each thought or belief you listed. For example, if you wrote, "I don't deserve to be rich," on the opposite side, write: "God's will for me is perfect abundance." If you wrote, "I'm not worthy of a perfect relationship," in the second column, write: "God's will for me is perfect partnership."

Once you've added God's vision next to your own, make a conscious decision to choose God's. You'll achieve this by using the power of your feelings, just as you did in the previous exercise. What emotion will you choose? Let it be joy! Read each of the items in the second column—those corresponding with the will of God—and use the feeling of joy to attract them into your life. Then just as before, initiate the feeling of gratitude, giving thanks for this new decision you've made, one that's in alignment with God's vision for you.

If you choose so, your life will begin to shift in this moment. *Let it be so, and it is.*

CHAPTER FIVE

REALITY VS. IMAGINATION

Ask yourself right now if you want to be a prisoner or if you wish to be free. No one in their right mind would pick captivity if the choice was put before them so clearly. But let's think about it for a moment. No one in their *right mind* would choose bondage, yet when you're honest with yourself, it's evident that until now, that has been your choice. Choosing to be weak and insufficient is a kind of prison. Is it possible then, that you haven't been in your right mind? What other possibility is there? The answer is simple: you've been thinking with your *split mind*.

A symptom of a split mind is the belief that you've been successful in splitting apart from God. From there, it's an easy jump to assert that you've also broken away from everything else—all the people you encounter, the world, and everything in it. Of course, the individuals around you will reflect the original decision you made about your relationship with God, which until now says that you're separate and alone. And if you're separate and alone, it also means you're vulnerable to attack, and thus, you're at war with everything around you.

Is any of this beginning to sound familiar?

A belief that isn't grounded in reality can't become real just because you want it to be. A thought may seem genuine and manifest in your life in different ways, but if it doesn't align with the will of God, then it has no real effect—and what has no real effect is not real.

This is called your imagination.

You can imagine any world you want, but if it exists only in your mind, then it isn't a real world. The only real world is the one that's supported by real laws, and real laws can only come from God—otherwise known as the "Creative Force of the Universe."

There was a time when most people on the planet believed that the world was flat. The collective decision about this so-called *flatness* was so profound that any seafaring journey was accompanied by extreme terror. What if you went too far and fell off the edge? This wisdom was never questioned; in fact, all evidence seemed to support the theory. You could stand on any beach in the world, look at the distant horizon, and actually see where the world ended. There it was, right in front of you . . . but does that make it real?

What do you think would have happened if you traveled back through time and told everyone the truth? You explain that the earth is actually round, and the apparent flatness is being caused by the curvature of the planet. How do you think people would react? Ask Galileo!

The news would probably not be welcomed, as history has shown that people who bear unfamiliar or unconventional insights are often forcibly brought back into line. After all, boundaries are comfortable when you're in prison—everyone knows where they stand and what's expected of them. It doesn't really matter if the decision is right or wrong, or if the evidence used to make the decision is flawed. What matters is the *idea,* for there's comfort in thinking you're right.

Over the last 12 years since *The Moses Code* was first released, there have been many, many people who laughed at or ridiculed this simple formula. They use the evidence that's readily available to assert a limited, ego-based vision that most people in the world would agree with. After all, it's easy to fall in line with what most people believe, even if it means denying the truth you feel moving within you. I felt a bit like Galileo myself! In spite of all this, there have been many more people—*you*, for example—who instinctively feel the "rightness" of the Code and everything being described in this book. For most people, just reading these pages releases a sense of freedom within, an energy that may not be supported by the logic of the world, but which you simply know is true.

Once again, thinking you're right doesn't make it so. If a thought doesn't align with reality, then it has no actual effect; and as I've said before, what has no effect isn't real. You can want it to be real, put energy into making it seem real, and wish with all your might, but some laws can't be overcome. If you're working against the Creative Force of the Universe, then all the wishing in the world isn't going to help you.

So let's get back to that Creative Force, also known as God. If the ego believes you're vulnerable, weak, and alone, but God believes the opposite, which one will you believe?

Exactly what does God say about you?

- You are holy.
- You are perfect.
- You are safe.

The abundance you seek comes from realizing these truths, not with your mind but with your whole heart. This is what the Moses Code offers you—the ability to align your will with the will of God by using his name. The more you practice these exercises, the more you'll embrace all of these gifts and share them with others. God only gives because everything that's given *by* God is given *to* God. Imitate this and there's nothing you can't accomplish.

Here's another way to look at God's role in all this. We like to think about God in a personal way, as if God is personally concerned about our well-being. This is true to a certain degree, but it goes deeper than you think. To me, God is "impersonal" rather than personal. God is mostly concerned with you realizing the Divine Power that sleeps within you. One of the ways that happens is by giving you everything you "really" ask for. In the previous chapter you read that God always gives you what you ask for simply because the power of God rests within you. Ask and it shall be given to you (Mt 7:7). So, when you ask for something that limits or even hurts you—it is given so you'll realize how much power your soul possesses. Every time you use the Code by saying, "I AM sad," the impersonal nature of God answers: "You're using My Name to be sad—and so it shall be." Every time you say, "I AM poor," the impersonal nature of God answers: "You're using My Name to seem poor—and so it shall be." This will happen over and over until you realize how much power you exert every time you use the Moses Code, consciously or unconsciously. When you finally get to the point where you use the name of God to claim that which serves your life rather than limits it, you'll be well on your way to freedom.

Exercise #5:
The Law of Giving and Receiving

If the nature of God is to give, then it would serve us well to imitate this action. In the past, most of us have focused our minds on *giving in order to receive*. In other words, behind every act of giving is the expectation of getting something. One of the problems with this way of thinking is that we usually believe we know exactly what it is we should receive, and therefore, we give to others as a way of bargaining for what we think we want. If we want our partner to rub our back, we may offer to rub theirs first. Now there's certainly nothing wrong with this, but it's time to explore an even higher way of giving to others that doesn't require bargaining.

What happens if you offer to rub your partner's back, who gladly accepts, but then doesn't offer to return the favor? If your favor was predicated on the desire to receive, then you'll probably be frustrated or even mad. "I rub your back all the time, and you never rub mine!" may be your response, and even if it isn't true, it appears that way to your ego. Why? Simply because the ego is concerned with only one thing: receiving. The idea of giving without motivation—except to imitate God—seems insane. "What's in it for me?" the ego asks. The answer is clear. What's in it for you is a gift far greater than a back rub or anything else you can imagine. What's in it for you is freedom.

Freedom from what? The motivation of your soul is to know that it's free to experience anything it chooses. If you want to experience bondage, then you're free to do so. However, if you wish to experience yourself as holy, a very different application must be applied. Since giving and receiving are ultimately the same thing, the only way to experience yourself as holy is to see others as holy. In other words, if you want to receive the gifts of God, you must give them away.

Wait a minute. Hasn't this entire section been centered on giving without expectation? How can you be free of expectation if you're seeing other people as holy in order to know yourself as holy?

71

I like to call this *Divine Selfishness*. The fact is that it's nearly impossible for us to exist without the ego or its motivations. The key isn't to destroy them but to use them in a new way—one that achieves the goals of your soul. There are things that each one of us desires such as peace, joy, contentment, and success, to name a few. If it's true that giving and receiving are the same, then it makes sense to give what we most want.

So if your highest goal is to be happy, make others feel that way. The more happiness you spread, the more you'll experience. This is using the ego in a new way, and it honors every part of you: your soul that seeks to give and your ego that seeks to receive.

Let's return to the back rub. Ask yourself, *Is getting my back massaged my real goal, or is there something deeper?* Perhaps what you really want is to feel loved and cared for, and that may not come from the person you're offering something to. The Universe might have a different plan for you—something you can't perceive at the moment you're offering a gift. You may give love and affection only to have it returned from a direction you didn't expect.

Spend some time today focusing on what you really want. It's certainly more than attaining a new car or some other possession. You may get these things, but if the soul is ignored, you won't come close to reaching genuine fulfillment, which the ego can never understand. Pick one quality that you choose to receive into your life today. Is it joy? Peace? Love? Now find creative ways to increase that quality in the life of someone who's close to you or even someone you've just met. Give this person what *you* desire, and then check within and see how you feel. Has the longing changed at all? Are you able to feel the quality that you helped inspire in another person?

Once you achieve this, you'll want to adjust your life in order to do this as much as you can. This is the secret that the ego has tried to keep you from discovering.

CHAPTER SIX

THE HOLY NAME OF GOD

When Moses told God that he could never accomplish the seemingly impossible goal of setting the Hebrews free (in fact, even the father of his religion would find such a job insurmountable), God had one simple answer:

> I appeared to Abraham, to Isaac, and to
> Jacob, by the name of God Almighty,
> but by my name was I not known to
> them. (Ex 6:3)

Abraham knew the Divine by a title—the title of "God Almighty." For the first time, however, God is known by an actual name: I AM THAT I AM. This indicates an intimacy that didn't exist until that moment. The question then becomes: Was this closeness reserved for Moses and the Hebrews, or was this a gift given to each one of us? The idea that God loves one group or person over the rest is very humanlike . . . that's what we do, but it isn't what God does.

God's love is unconditional, and the name of God, indicating intimacy or oneness, is a gift bestowed upon everyone. So what should we do with it? Do we shrink away like Moses did at first, saying that we're not worthy? Do we use it once or twice, witness the power of the Sacred Name, and then file it away in a neat little tabernacle never to be seen again? Or could we use it to change our lives and the world?

THE COMMANDMENT

Over the years I've had the chance to bring many groups to Israel, the land promised to Moses and the Hebrew people. On a recent trip, we spent time in a small town called Safed, which is renowned as the greatest center for Kabbalah, one of the most mystical, spiritual paths in the world. While visiting a gift store, I spotted a sculpture behind the counter with the Hebrew letters that spelled the name of God. I asked the young woman working there if she'd pronounce it in Hebrew for me.

"That would be breaking one of the commandments of God," she replied matter-of-factly, as if any child would know. "God said we should never take the holy name in vain, and that's why it must not be pronounced."

I explained that I was raised with the same commandment but with a very different understanding of what it meant. Christians are taught that taking the Lord's name in vain is an edict to not swear or curse, but it seemed that she had a much more literal interpretation.

"No, that's not what it means at all," she said. "It's one of the clearest things we learn, and it's right there in black and white. Taking God's name in vain means we can't pronounce it at all. If we do, terrible things will happen to us."

I asked her where she learned this and if it was a common Jewish belief.

"It has nothing to do with being common," she continued. "This is the truth, and there's no way to interpret around it. If you say the name of God, then sometime in the future, he'll remember it and punish you. There is a way to avoid this, though."

Of course I was intrigued.

"We sometimes change one of the letters so that we can say it without really saying it. If I wanted to say your name, James, but you asked me not to, I might say Yames instead. That way, I'm safe and haven't done anything wrong."

I realized that this is what happened to the Hebrews when they left Egypt and began searching for the land that God provided for them. They were empowered by the Holy Name, but it was ultimately set aside.

Was this what God had intended, or was it the result of fear?

There's nothing in the Torah that specifically prohibits Jews from pronouncing the name of God. In fact, it's clear from many ancient sources that God's name was spoken aloud routinely, especially when praying in the temple. The Mishnah—an early written compilation of Jewish oral tradition that became the basis of the Torah—recommends using God's name as a routine greeting (Berakhot 9:5). However, by the time of the Talmud, the custom was to substitute names for God. Some rabbis even taught that a person who pronounces the actual name instead of using a substitute should be put to death (what nearly happened to Jesus). Things had certainly shifted in a new direction.

It's also interesting to note that the version of the name of God we're using for the Moses Code is actually a misinterpretation of the original Hebrew text. For years, perhaps even centuries, most of us were led to trust the most popular translation of God's words—the original name given to Moses, I AM THAT I AM. Many esoteric schools have borrowed and promoted this translation, some even using it as the foundation of their teaching.

The actual Hebrew words that God used when speaking to Moses were "EHYEH ASHER EHYEH," which when properly translated means, "I will be who I will be." God actually spoke to Moses in the future tense, not the present. The question then becomes, How does this fact influence or deny our use of the mistranslation, especially as it applies to using the Holy Name as a tool for manifestation?

God exists in all places at all times. If this is true, then God lives in the past, present, and future all at once. This is something that most people who have any degree of faith or belief in God can accept, so it doesn't need to be argued here. However, it does have a great deal of significance in settling this potential dispute.

Referring to people in the past tense is the same as referring to them in the present tense; in other words, the individual whom we're talking about hasn't changed. When we say, "Bob was here," we're referring to the same person as when we say, "Bob is here."

Therefore, if we say, "I WILL BE WHO I WILL BE," knowing that we're referring to the Reality we sometimes call God, it's no different from saying, "I AM THAT I AM." As my friend Jonathan Goldman, one of the best-known sound healers in the world, states: "Sound plus intention creates healing."

The words on their own mean very little without the intention. It's the intent that calls the Spirit of God into the equation, and it's where we find the real mystery.

Going back to the young woman I met in the shop in Safed, her attempt to avoid God's judgment by substituting a letter in the name or saying it with a different inflection was without effect. Changing a letter or two in any name doesn't alter the intention, and this—more than anything else—is what creates the Divine Link.

So why are we placing any importance on the Sacred Name at all?

Knowing someone's name amplifies your connection with that person. You can call me James or Jimmy—I'll respond to either one. However, each of these names carries a different energy and may cause me to respond in various ways. James is used in formal settings, as an author or when I'm giving a presentation or concert. Jimmy is what many of my friends call me; it's more intimate and playful. But I love them both, and ultimately, it makes little difference which one is used if I feel a connection with the person using it.

Is it possible that God is the same?

———✦———

Let's look at this a bit deeper. Knowing the name of God allows you to create an intimate connection with the Divine rather than something out of reach or distant. It's the intimacy we're concerned with here. When you realize that you are one with God, rather than separate and sinful, then it's easy to feel and extend that closeness. Many of us were raised with the image of an "old white man in the clouds" image of God. This is both immature and insulting. For hundreds or even thousands of years, people from European backgrounds wanted to dominate other cultures and seem superior. How many paintings of Jesus have you seen where he is depicted as a white man as opposed to the truth of his appearance—a dark-skinned man from the Middle East? Not only do these images of God separate us—painting God as unreachable—but they exclude most of the world's population. If we are to experience the intimacy and immediacy of God, we need to set all those strange images aside and approach God as the Beloved.

God gave Moses the Holy Name to secure the Hebrews' release from slavery. In doing so, an intimacy was established between God and humanity that had never existed before that time. Imagine that you meet someone and want to become friends. You give the person your name and trust that he or she will use it whenever they need anything. How would you feel if the individual decided that your love is too great and they're unworthy of using it? The intention isn't to join but to remain separate or apart, and this becomes the result. When we call upon the name of God in either the past, present, or future tense with the intention of joining, a connection is created that allows us to create miracles. This is the essence of the Moses Code.

So whether you use I AM THAT I AM or I WILL BE WHO I WILL BE, the result is the same. The intention of connecting with the Divine combined with the name creates an intimacy with God that unites you with the Creator's main function. And what is the function of God?

To create!

This is the purpose of the book: for you to realize once and for all that God's function and yours are the same. You're here to be a creative force of peace and harmony. Just as you respond to the variations of your own name, treating them the same and tuning in to the intention, so does God respond to you when your heart is open and your intention clear.

Exercise #6:
The Second Form

Until now, you've been using the Moses Code chant to attract into your life everything you hold in your heart. It's important to remember, though, that we can only truly have something if we're willing to offer it to another. In other words, we must be willing to share the gifts of God.

To learn this energetically, we're going to reverse the movement of the chant. Instead of breathing out on the phrase "I AM THAT," begin by saying those words on the in breath. As you do this, make sure that you *feel* the energy of the quality you're integrating. For example, if your goal is to spread compassion, then get a strong sense of how you feel when you're compassionate. Think, *I AM that compassion*, and feel the emotion run through your entire body.

Now exhale, saying aloud: "I AM." As you do so, feel that quality extending outward, touching every person and living being wherever they are. Remember that our primary goal in using the Moses Code is to actually act as God would on Earth—in other words, to give as God gives. As I've said many times already, God gives unconditionally all the time. If it is God's function

> to give, then it is ours as well. Use this adapted
> chant to actually sense what it feels like to spread
> light, happiness, and joy throughout the world.

FINAL THOUGHTS FOR PART I

God's will for you is perfect joy. Think about
that for a moment. Perfect joy means total joy, and
everything you desire is included in that. But it also
indicates something higher, a level of joy that transcends this world. It means that God wants you to
be abundant and successful and have a perfect relationship, but it also signifies that there are realities
beyond the physical that you can also claim.

Jesus said:

> Seek first God's kingdom and God's
> righteousness, and all these things will
> be added to you. (Mt 6:33)

He didn't tell us to search for the riches of the
world in order to be happy. In fact, he said something very different. Jesus advised that we seek after
the riches of Heaven, which are invulnerable to the
spoils of time. The material wealth of the world can
never fill the void we feel within us. If God's will
for us is perfect joy, then there must be something

more—there must be a deeper call beyond this physical realm that gives us what we really need.

Together, we'll travel there next. You've learned how to harness the power of the name of God to attract everything you want in the world. Now we'll use it to focus our attention on the gifts that extend beyond the limitations of this world. This was God's intention all along. Earthly riches were nothing more than an introduction to the real gifts that are waiting for us. The good thing is that you don't have to die in order to receive them. Many people believe they can only experience perfect joy in Heaven, and Heaven is a place you can go to only after you've died. Yet didn't Jesus say, "The Kingdom of God is within you" (Luke 17:21)?

The Kingdom of Heaven is within you, waiting to be expressed everywhere you go. Every breath you take, every move you make is an opportunity to extend Heaven and the gifts of God to the people around you. That's what God does, and imitating this is more than the greatest form of flattery . . . it's your salvation.

PART II

The Real
Journey
Begins

A WORD OF CAUTION
FROM THE AUTHOR

I hope you'll pay close attention to what you're about to read and understand that I'm being literal and quite serious. If you choose to continue exploring these teachings after you've read this note, then you'll be doing so at your own risk. You may decide to stop here and apply everything you've learned until now; and if you do, I assure you that your life will be wonderful. You've already gained enough information to "turn everything around"—in fact, nothing will ever be the same from this moment on. You can use the Moses Code to attract wealth beyond your imagination, abundance that you've only dreamed of, and everything else your heart desires. If you stop right now and simply use everything you've learned, you'll be a shining example to everyone you encounter, showing them a new possibility in life. You've already come so far, and no one would fault you if you decide to end the journey here.

But there's still a great distance to go—information and experiences that your mind can't even begin to fathom. If you choose to remain on this path just a bit longer, I guarantee that everything will change. *Everything!* In fact, what you've learned

up until now is just a fraction of what awaits you
. . . if you're willing. All I can say is that you must
be committed and serious if you wish to embark on
the rest of this journey. It isn't meant for the faint of
heart but for those who are willing to risk everything
for the chance to *be* everything.

Are you still with me?

It's as if we've been walking through a magical
forest and have suddenly come to a fork in the path.
One leads in the direction foretold at the beginning
of this book, offering you the ability to attract everything you desire into your life. I mean that quite literally. Once it's understood and practiced, the Code
gives you the means to produce miracles in your life
and the world, and there's no limit to how far you
can go. If that's what you want, then it's what you
will certainly achieve.

Let's imagine that this path leads to the left. If
you have any question at all about whether or not
you should continue, then I suggest you take it. Put
this book down and begin working with the exercises and information. Commit yourself to using
the power inherent in the name of God to attract
everything you can imagine in your mind. There's
no more advice you need in order to do so, because
everything already exists within.

However, there's another path that lies before us, one that leads in a new direction you haven't yet traveled. This path is much narrower than what you've experienced so far, and the canopy of trees overhead makes the forest seem dark and even a bit dangerous. I guarantee that this isn't an illusion. It *is* more dangerous, and the life you've known up until now is in great peril if you choose to continue. I don't mean that you could be physically hurt or die if you venture down this path and are unable to finish. I know I'm being dramatic, but my description isn't that over the top. What you may lose is far more important and valuable than your physical life, and this is what you must examine.

Here's the other thing you should know: if you decide to press on, the life that I'm describing here will be lost either way, at one point or another. The path we've been walking—even as it forks in two different directions—circles back on itself and ends exactly where it began. In other words, the ending is inevitable. All I'm offering you is a quicker and more direct route, one that will allow you to avoid untold sorrow and heartache.

Yes, I mean exactly what I just wrote. The path to the left—the one that leads in what may at first seem like the safe passage—will never satisfy you. It's true that it will allow you to attract amazing wealth and abundance, but what you'll discover in the end is that those things aren't what you're really looking for. You're truly seeking what the path to the right offers, which can only mean that either direction has its own dangers. The "left" path may seem safe, but in the end you can't avoid the lessons you were born to learn; the "right" path requires a level of commitment you haven't yet experienced.

Which one will you choose?

If you're still reading, then I'll assume that you've decided to continue our journey toward awakening. From this point on, you'll walk to a world that your mind can't comprehend but your heart already perceives. You've realized that it's the only thing that will satisfy you. Most of all, you'll know that you're ready for this step, and that the Moses Code will give you everything your heart truly desires.

From here, you walk on toward eternity. . . .

CHAPTER SEVEN

THE TWO PATHS

God loves a clear and resolute decision. It means that you've considered all the options, weighed the costs and benefits from both sides, and made an absolute choice to move forward. Now that you've decided to step into the deeper levels of the Moses Code, angels will come to support you. Let's continue on this path into worlds you've only imagined until now.

Begin by visualizing yourself standing at the fork in the path. Put one foot in front of the other, and start heading toward the path that leads to the right. The passage immediately becomes narrower, and it's difficult to see where it leads. Yet within your heart you feel exhilarated, for you know that this decision will lead to a greater understanding of the Moses Code—one that satisfies the soul's longing rather than the ego's.

At last we've defined the difference between these two courses. The path we've walked on until now, which continues to the left, leads to the fulfillment of the ego's desires (the part of you that believes itself to be separate from God and everything else), while the path to the right leads to the fulfillment of the soul's longing.

What's the difference?

Let's begin with the ego. Here are a few of the characteristics of this elusive state of consciousness:

- The ego believes that everything is separate from everything else that it perceives. In other words, you're split apart from the person sitting next to you, the house in which you live, the world that supports your existence, and the Universe that contains all life. Of course in the end, and most especially, you are separate from God.

- Because you're isolated and alone, you must find a way to defend your life from all the other things that may and probably will attack you. If you don't, then something—at one point or another—is going to come along and claim you. This is what the ego calls death.

- Since death is the only thing that the ego is completely sure of, it must live in fear. It's afraid of almost everything because there's no way to know which part of the "separate" Universe will attempt to claim its life.

- One way to ward off death, at least for a little while, is to gather as much *stuff* as possible. Anything that seems to have value will do, but the ego prefers the *big stuff.* The grander the house, the more comfortable the ego feels—until, of course, it realizes that nothing can secure its life. It keeps searching, hoping to find the next big thing that might keep it alive. But in the end, everything fails no matter how grandiose, and the ego dies as surely as everything else it created and perceives.

Now let's examine the characteristics of your soul:

- The soul never seeks to *get* anything, because it knows that it already possesses everything of value, and whatever lacks value is disregarded, given little, if any, attention. Why? Because the soul knows that everything flows easily and naturally in its direction when it's aligned with its Divine Source. Abundance, ideal relationships, and security aren't the goals but are achieved without effort.

- Whereas the ego seeks to *get,* believing that it then possesses whatever it needs, the soul seeks to *give,* knowing that its needs are already fulfilled.

- The soul understands that death isn't real, because whatever is real can't be injured or threatened in any way. Fear, therefore, is overcome because the soul knows itself to be invulnerable, perfectly protected from any perceived threat or error.

It goes without saying that the ego—with all its defenses and desires—isn't real, or at the very least, it's a shadow of reality. Yet we've built our entire existence on believing in this illusion, putting all our faith in its assertions and endowing it with its own world where it can conquer and rule.

Imagine that you're standing in a room with a single bright light set to one side. The light hits your body and casts a shadow on the floor, roughly the same shape as your body. If you were to stand in this room for a very long time, or if something were to happen that robs you of your memory, you may be tempted to forget the body and the light and focus entirely on the shadow, giving it a life that doesn't really exist. The shape is no longer that of your body but of a creature or monster that may attack you at any moment. Every time you move, it moves, too, although you're unable to perceive the relationship because you've forgotten that your body and the shadow are actually the same. You become afraid of the body that created the shadow and especially fear the light that created them both.

But do the shadow and all the things that you've decided it represents exist? Wouldn't it be more accurate to say that it's a projection of reality, or a manifestation of blocked light? And what of the body—what role does it play in this analogy?

The body that casts the shadow is your soul, more tangible and real than all the projections the ego claims. And this leads us to the point of no return. What I'm about to share may be harder to grasp than anything else you've read in this book, yet it's the last remaining ingredient toward understanding and using the Moses Code. This is our final destination—where this and every path ultimately leads. If you're able to accept this single fact, then reality itself will fall in all around you.

The body that casts the shadow—what we're now calling the soul—is no more real than the shadow itself.

This understanding, that what you call your soul is not ultimately real, is a very difficult concept to grasp. Isn't the soul eternal? Yes, but not as something that is separate or distinct from God. You might believe that you have a soul and that the person next to you also has a soul, and that they're somehow distinct from each other. And this is the subtle point we're trying to make—there is only one soul, and it's the soul we share. You've heard it said that giving and receiving are the same, and most of us are willing to accept that statement as true. But why is it true? It's true because "Everything I give to thee is received by me." I can't give anything to you without receiving it myself. Hold on to this for now, because I don't want you to try to figure it out in your mind. That's actually the best way to become even more confused. It would be better to accept the possibility of this truth, then let the truth itself reveal itself as we move forward.

In the end, only the light (that is, God) exists and preexists everything. Your goal is to touch, embrace, and finally absorb this reality and then project it into every aspect of your life. But in order to accomplish this task, you must take it one step at a time, for there's no way to rush this transformation. It will occur in three stages. For now, I'll refer to them as the:

1. Shadow, representing the ego

2. Body, representing the soul

3. Light, representing God

A little later in this book, you'll redefine these once again, returning to the biblical story of Moses's conversation with God. It's a dialogue you're having even now, in every moment of your life. God is offering you the entire answer, although until this moment, you've been unable to consider the full impact of what you've heard. It's been easier to listen to only a small part of the message: what has served the decisions you've already made about yourself, your life, and everything you desire. It's time to lay them all aside, for where you'll venture to now is uncharted territory—at least from the perspective of the ego.

The terrain may be different from what you've imagined, but it leads to the home you've never left except in your imagination. But your mind can't make concrete what has no genuine substance. It can only make it *seem* real, but what seems real can never replace what is. This is where the Moses Code leads.

Let's move on to the *real* world. . . .

Exercise #7:
What Your Soul Really Wants

Begin by making a list of everything that your soul longs for. For example, some of the things you write down may include: peace, love, joy, or compassion. Your goal is to unlock the doors that they hide behind in order to share them with others—thereby realizing that they were within you and already yours.

Use the Moses Code to stimulate the *feeling* of each of the qualities you've listed. If you're wanting to unlock the experience of love, chant on the in breath: "I AM THAT LOVE." Feel it filling your entire being. As you exhale, say aloud, "I AM," and sense that God—along with you—is extending this into the world. Stay with the chant until you begin to feel the quality fully alive and present in your life. Then move on to the next item on your list.

This process is a powerful tool for awakening the traits that your soul has been longing for but have always lived hidden within you. When you're finished with this exercise, sit for a few moments in silence and see if you can sense a different energy. Do you feel fulfilled in a way that evades your ego's understanding? If so, you're on the right track!

CHAPTER EIGHT

SPIRITUAL VS. RELIGIOUS

In 1995, a book was published that shocked many people around the globe. *Conversations with God,* by Neale Donald Walsch, sat at the number one position on *The New York Times* bestseller list for more than two years, and the publishing world hasn't been the same since. Many people hadn't considered the possibility that God never stopped speaking to humanity and that anyone could have an intimate encounter with the Divine Presence—sometimes known as God—anytime they chose. It was assumed that God only spoke to the greatest prophets and teachers that we've read about in the Bible or other sacred texts, but the idea that God would speak to an ordinary person living today seemed impossible.

But as we're discovering now, nothing is impossible, especially when it comes to this topic.

The story that led Neale to his own Divine encounter is probably not terribly different from your own. It was at a time when Neale seemed to have lost everything of value in his life. He was at the lowest rung on the ladder when he heard a voice from within—a voice he recognized but couldn't believe. It was the voice of God; and a conversation began that changed the way we look at ourselves, the world, and our connection with the Creator.

How many times have you felt lost and out of control but then sensed a gentle voice within assuring you that everything would be fine? We usually assume that this is a conversation with our own self, perhaps a higher part of us that lies just beyond the reach of our conscious mind. If we could only remember that this is exactly correct and that there is no distance between our Higher Self and God, then perhaps we'd realize that we're conversing with the Divine every moment of our lives. It's as if the phone line between God and ourselves is always open, and God is waiting to be included in the conversation. Instead, we continue on our way, thinking that we're alone and able to control the endless details of our lives without our Divine Benefactor's influence.

But what happens when we remember this connection and tap into its wisdom for everything we think, say, or do?

God is in every detail of your life, guiding you into the infinite reality in which you were created and still remain. Let's stop there for a moment, because it's so important; in fact, the first sentence of this paragraph may be the most crucial assertion in the book. We'll break it apart and look at it piece by piece.

God is in every detail of your life.

This is something that most people, if they have any concept of God at all, have no problem accepting. The whole point of a religious life is to see the Divine thumbprint in every moment, knowing that God is in charge and watching over us. Notice that I used the word *religious* instead of *spiritual*. I could have just as easily written "the whole point of a spiritual life," but this wouldn't have conveyed what I'm trying to illustrate.

So what's the difference between a religious person and a spiritual person? I'll begin by repeating something that a friend told me many years ago. He said: "The difference is that a religious person believes in hell while a spiritual person has been there." It may be cute, but in some ways it's true. What are some of the other possible differences?

- Religious people oftentimes believe that God is "out there" somewhere, usually in Heaven, whereas spiritual people know that there's no separation between themselves and their Divine Source.

- Religious people may believe that they must die before they can enter Heaven, and spiritual people trust that Jesus was correct when he said: "The Kingdom of God is within you."

- Religious people sometimes state that God is holy and they are not, whereas spiritual people know that anything created by God is still one with God. Therefore, if the Creator is holy, so are they. As it says in 1 Corinthians: "Know ye not that ye are the Temple of God and that the Spirit dwells within you?"

- Religious people may believe that God's love is conditional and can be taken away at any moment, but spiritual people know that God's love is eternal and unconditional.

I'm being careful to say that these are statements a religious person *sometimes* believes but not always. I'm fully aware that it's possible to be spiritual and religious at the same time. What I'm really trying to convey is that spiritual individuals "experience" God in a way that transcends thought and logic, and their experience of the Divine isn't limited to any one religious or spiritual tradition. The deeper one goes into the spiritual experience, the more universal it becomes. Christian theologians may draw profound distinctions between their beliefs and those of Muslims, Jews, or even from other sects of Christianity. A Christian mystic, on the other hand, quickly experiences the meaninglessness of these schisms and watches calmly as all divergent streams flow into the same ocean.

This is in no way intended to regard people who attend a particular church or religion as wrong or disadvantaged. I'm personally very active in my own church and consider myself to be a committed Christian. However, I am not limited by any form but am able to move effortlessly between them all. If you resonate with a particular religion—great. The key is to follow that religion to the very core and not stay on the surface. Every religion has its mystics, or people who transcend the surface practices of their faith and dive to the very center. The interesting thing you find is that the closer you get to the center, the more you realize that all religions are guiding us to the same experience.

A VIEW FROM ABOVE

Do you remember the story of the astronauts who first saw our planet from outer space? Their perspective of the world changed when they gazed upon it, seeing past the boundaries and divisions that rule our lives. Borders that separate countries mean very little to one who views Earth in its entirety—much like the mystic who rises above the divergent beliefs of a particular religion only to see that all paths ultimately lead to God.

The second part of the sentence we're examining says: ". . . guiding you into the infinite reality in which you were created and still remain."

Ah, this is something very different from what most of us were taught in Sunday school or catechism class. When I was growing up in the Catholic Church, I never heard anything about remaining perfect as I was created. In fact, I was told the opposite—we're born in sin and need to be redeemed through a wonderful sacrament called baptism. If you die before you're baptized—so the story says—then straight to hell you'll descend to burn for all eternity, which, by the way, is a very long time.

I felt little solace when I was told that God had a special place for children who die before they have the chance to be baptized. Apparently, Limbo is just between Heaven and hell and was created especially for these poor infants. While they'll never see God, at least they won't suffer eternal hellfire—a small consolation from a merciful God.

This leads to the ultimate difference between a spiritual and a religious person: a religious person sometimes believes that we were born in sin and need to be redeemed, while a spiritual person knows that redemption isn't required. In other words, you're perfect as you were created, and there's nothing you can do to change the love that is your Source. Most Christians believe that the role of Jesus was to redeem our sins and reunite us with our Divine Inheritance. A spiritual person, on the other hand, recognizes that Jesus's role was to demonstrate the true meaning of love by conquering death, showing us the infinite potential not only of his soul, but of ours as well.

Now a true conversation can begin, one that isn't predicated on inequality and disparity, but on union and love. And this is where the Moses Code fits in. When God spoke to Moses in the form of the burning bush, he established a link between Heaven and Earth that hadn't existed before that moment. God told Moses the Holy Name. That may not sound like a momentous occasion from our perspective, but from the perspective of Moses and the Israelites, it was.

It's hard to have a conversation with someone whose name you don't know. If you only know a title—in this case, it's "God Almighty" or even "the God of Our Forefathers"—then no intimacy can be established. Intimacy, after all, is the purpose of communion, which is the ultimate result of a deep conversation.

Moses opened the door for humanity to have an intimate conversation with the Divine. Centuries after Moses, another Jewish leader, King Solomon, wrote about God as a lover and intimate partner. His ecstatic relationship with the Divine wasn't perceived as unreachable and unapproachable, but as a spouse whose presence makes him drunk with love.

> *Let him kiss me with the kisses of his mouth—*
> *for thy love is better than wine.*

(SONG OF SONGS 1:2)

Mystics from every tradition have echoed these emotions, experiencing the Divine less in the mind and more in the heart. In Christianity, saints such as Teresa of Ávila, John of the Cross, and Francis of Assisi have shared splendid accounts of their rapture; and in Sufism, few have ever reached the heights of Rumi when he wrote:

I swallowed
some of the Beloved's sweet wine,
and now I am ill.

My body aches,
my fever is high.

They called in the Doctor and he said,
drink this tea!

Ok, time to drink this tea.
Take these pills!

Ok, time to take these pills.
The Doctor said,
get rid of the sweet wine of his lips!

Ok, time to get rid of the doctor.

God is wine, and upon this sweet drink we've become drunkards, losing our former selves and discovering our true nature that's holy and worthy of an embrace the world can never comprehend. God has moved from the unnamed to the named and, ultimately, to the Beloved.

The question then becomes: Is God moving toward us, or are we moving toward God? If we believe that God moves closer to humanity as the centuries progress, then we must also think that God's love is conditional. In other words, the more God gets to know us, the more affection flows in our direction. But this reflects human relationships more accurately than it does the Divine. From the perspective of Divinity, God only gives to God. We hold back our giving until we're sure it's going to be accepted and then returned. If this is true, then perhaps there's something to be learned from our newfound intimacy with God. Perhaps it's finally time to begin imitating God rather than expecting our Creator to imitate us.

What does it mean to say that God only gives? This is impossible from a human perspective, because if we believe that we're giving our energy or resources away to people who exist outside of us, there comes a point where we have nothing left to give. If we offered up all our energy, we'd die . . . then where would we be? Our idea of giving is: "Know your limit; don't give more than you can afford to lose."

Let's shift perspectives so that we can understand how God gives.

Most of us are willing to consider the possibility that God doesn't perceive separation. In other words, everything is contained within the whole we sometimes call God, and there's nothing outside that whole. Physics teaches us that energy can't be created or destroyed; it moves from one place to another. If this is so, then anything we give to another person is really nothing more than an exchange of energy, but from God's perspective, it really hasn't gone anywhere. Simply put, the energy hasn't left its source, which is God. God is the source of all energy, and therefore it can never leave or go anywhere at all. It remains where it has always been, even though it may seem to move from one person or situation to another.

Welcome to a new world!

This leaves us with only one possibility. Giving and receiving aren't two different experiences but one—they are the same.

Oh Divine Master,
grant that I may not so much seek to be consoled
as to console,
To be understood as to understand,
To be loved as to love;

For it is in giving that we receive,
It is in pardoning that we are pardoned,
And it is in dying that we are born to eternal life.

— FRANCIS OF ASSISI

The purpose of the Moses Code is to experience the intimacy of our relationship with the Divine and then spread it to others. We're here to imitate God, but we can't do it unless we understand our Creator. Understanding comes only from relating to or communicating with someone or something, and we can only deeply communicate with someone if we know the person. The gift that Moses gave us, then, was the Holy Name and since then, we've been moving closer to God rather than expecting God to move closer to us.

Exercise #8:
Conversing with God

It's time to enter into this conversation more intimately, just as Moses did. Up to this point, you've been using the Moses Code to either attract the things that you don't presently possess into your life or to extend into the world the more essential qualities that the soul is longing for. Now you'll use the Code to amplify and expand the holy connection between you and the Source, also known as God.

In this exercise, you can choose to either breathe in or breathe out on the "I AM THAT" phrase. There may be times when it feels more appropriate to exhale when saying this, drawing whatever you've focused on into your life. On other occasions, it may be better to use the chant to extend energy, so you begin by inhaling as you repeat the words. For now, it won't matter, because the goal of this exercise is different from anything else you've practiced here.

Your goal is to feel like you're *conversing with God* just as Moses did. Let your focus be the intimacy of this dialogue. As you utter the words "I AM THAT," feel that you're literally the connection between Heaven and Earth. And as you say, "I AM," sense that God is answering you, affirming this bond. Continue this exercise until you realize that you're completely one with God, sharing a level of intimacy that your logical mind can't comprehend.

CHAPTER NINE

THE TRICKLE-DOWN THEORY OF ENLIGHTENMENT

It may seem strange to apply one of the foundations of Reaganomics to the Moses Code, but it helps us understand the essential difference between the longing of the ego and the yearning of the soul. The ego seeks its own comfort, accumulating goods and money in the fruitless attempt to ward off death. In other words, it seeks to *get* as much as possible and use everything as a barricade against its inevitable demise. The soul, on the other hand, seeks to *give* as much as possible because it knows that it isn't limited by separation or death, and it can only realize this through giving away what it most desires.

You can't give what you don't have. The soul understands this; therefore, it gives everything all the time.

Mother Teresa once wrote, "When I am hungry give me someone I can feed, and when I am thirsty give me someone I can give a drink to."

She understood that the Prayer of St. Francis was right . . .

> to be loved as to love; For it is in giving that
> we receive . . . And it is in dying that we
> are born to eternal life.

This is the essential difference: the ego seeks to *get* while the soul seeks to *give*.

If you learn only one thing from this book, the above statement would be enough. Your soul longs to "give" everything because it knows that you are only giving to yourself. Your soul—or who you really are— knows that there is "no other." It sees and serves only God through every person or situation you encounter. The ego, on the other hand, has one goal: to separate from the inseparable. It does this by isolating itself and seeking to "get" what it doesn't really need.

The first stage of the Moses Code (what I'm calling the Shadow, which represents the ego) uses this powerful tool of manifestation to gather or get all the things that it thinks it needs and doesn't already possess. Let's be clear right from the beginning: there's absolutely nothing wrong with this! In fact, it's a necessary step in the process of awakening, but let's also clarify that it's only the first step. It may be tempting to look at those who've mastered this technique—who seem to have attained everything they've ever wanted—and think that they've reached the promised land of abundance and wealth. Unfortunately, mastering the initial step without comprehending the rest does little in satisfying the real longing, which can only be fulfilled by the soul.

The soul doesn't worry about the things it knows will come automatically once a higher level has been achieved. It's concerned only with the qualities and gifts that are eternal and beyond the physical world: peace, love, compassion, and gentleness. It focuses on the benevolence of Spirit, knowing that the gifts of the world will flow easily once a higher goal is sought.

Jesus said:

> Lay not up for yourselves treasures upon earth,
> where moth and rust do corrupt, and where
> thieves break through and steal. But lay up for

> yourselves treasures in heaven, where neither
> moth nor rust do corrupt, and where thieves
> do not break through nor steal. For where
> your treasure is, there will your heart be also.
> (Mt 6:19–21)

I like to call this the trickle-down theory of enlightenment. Jesus is saying that only eternal gifts are worthy of your attention, and he's also affirming that when you focus on these gifts, the rest are given to you automatically. He further states:

> Take no thought, saying, "What will we eat?"
> or "What will we drink?" or "How will we be
> clothed?" . . . Your heavenly Father knows that
> you have all these needs. Seek first the Kingdom
> of God, and his righteousness, and all these
> things shall be added unto you. (Mt 6:31–33)

In other words, when you seek after the highest level, everything beneath it is secured without effort. The key is to pursue the very highest gift the Universe can offer—what Jesus is calling the Kingdom of God. The things you need to sustain your life, house, income, and clothing—all of which are energetically less potent—flow easily and naturally into your life because, once again, God's will for you is perfect joy.

THE PYRAMID OF DESIRES

Visualize a pyramid broken up into many levels or stages. We'll call this the "Pyramid of Desires." At the very highest level—the top of the pyramid—is Heaven, or the Kingdom of God. The next level might be a desire for a life filled with love and peace; beneath that could be wishes for financial abundance. Only you can map out where these levels or desires will fall on your personal pyramid.

Now imagine achieving the highest goal—that is, the realization of Heaven on Earth at this moment, not after you die. The goal is to experience heavenly gifts in the here and now, and the energy of this will then begin to trickle down to the lower levels of your pyramid. After you've reached Heaven on Earth, the energy will fill the second level, a life filled with love and peace. Once this is fulfilled, it will then flow into financial abundance and then every subsequent level after that. You'll begin to realize that God's plan brings success to every area of your life—not just the initial desire.

What happens if you strive after and focus on one of the lower levels—for example, the desire for financial abundance? Let's imagine that you use the Moses Code, the power inherent in the name of God, to achieve it. Because the Universe always gives you everything you ask for, you easily attain the goal, and your bank account is suddenly overflowing with money. And since the trickle-down theory of enlightenment is also in effect, everything beneath this desire is also fulfilled. You're able to buy all the toys you think you need in order to be even happier than you are now. You also have a level of influence that allows you to climb the social ladder.

But what about the things that are positioned above financial abundance in your pyramid? You may have all the money you hoped to earn, but your family life is a disaster and you have no peace. Most of all, you've been unable to achieve the Kingdom of God, which is what your soul really wants. That's why no matter how much money you have, you're still not satisfied. At first you think that you simply need more of the thing you focused on (in this case, money). But no matter how much money you earn— even if you become the richest person on Earth—the feeling of dissatisfaction persists.

> What good will it be for a man if he gains the whole world, yet forfeits his soul? (Mt 16:26)

The fulfillment of the soul is your only desire, but you haven't realized this . . . perhaps until now. It may be impossible to permanently forfeit your soul, but you can ignore it. However, you can't neglect it forever. The longing of the soul becomes more and more persistent until you can no longer deny its call. Ignoring your soul ultimately becomes so painful that you have no other choice than to seek after the Kingdom of God or settle for an unsatisfied life. You may end up with an amazing house, the fastest car, and tremendous influence, but the most important things are still missing. It's as if God created a fail-safe system to ensure your final acceptance of the truth.

This is the truth we seek, and the Moses Code is the path we'll walk on toward our ultimate reward. It's time for us to recognize that our only goal is to imitate the gifts of God, as well as the generosity of God; and in doing so, we'll realize that we already have everything that our soul needs to be happy and completely satisfied. God only gives, yet everything is perfectly received by God. A gift can never truly leave its source, and this is what leads to our final acceptance of the Kingdom of God that lives within us.

Sharing these lessons around the world for over a decade, I found the trickle-down theory of enlightenment to be one of the most helpful tools in putting the Code into practice. Most of us were taught to put our attention on manifesting goods rather than goodness, or on wealth instead of well-being. This theory presents one of the highest mysteries in the Universe—when you seek after the highest level, everything else comes to you easily and automatically. You can call it anything you want—Heaven, the Kingdom, etc.—but what you'll discover is the high frequency at the top of the pyramid. St. Paul called this "The peace that surpasses all understanding" (Philippians 4:7).

Exercise #9:
Your Own Pyramid of Desires

Draw your own pyramid representing the trickle-down theory of enlightenment. Make it big enough so that you can write down a few words in each level. Start at the top—the pinnacle of the triangle. How would you describe what Jesus called the Kingdom of God, Heaven, enlightenment, and perfect love? Write those words at the very top. Now go to the bottom of the pyramid and list some of the things that you need to survive, such as food, clothing, and shelter. These are the most basic requirements of your life. You can focus on creating abundance here, or you can trust that the higher you rise on the pyramid, the more you can accept from God.

What are some of the gifts you could manifest directly above your most basic needs? Perhaps the next level for you would be satisfying your emotional needs or desires. Jot down a few of these just above the bottom level. How many more levels can you think of? Other than your physical or emotional needs, what else can you add to your pyramid? Take some time to write these in as much detail as possible, and then decide where you really want to focus. Remember that according to the trickle-down theory, everything below what you focus upon will automatically be created, while everything above it will be forgotten. For example, if you focus only on your physical needs, then everything above that position on your pyramid will be left unsatisfied.

After you've completed your pyramid, make a conscious effort to stay focused and create from the highest level possible. Your only goal should be attaining the Kingdom of Heaven, fully knowing that by staying true to this, all your other goals will be automatically realized.

CHAPTER TEN

SEEING
AS GOD SEES

The Shadow (the initial level of the Moses Code) seeks to use the power inherent in the name of God, I AM THAT I AM, to attract all the things that the ego believes it doesn't have, which will subsequently enrich your life. This is actually the first step in spiritual mastery: the realization that within you lies the power of the Universe, or God, and that you can do anything you want with it. If you wish to attract amazing wealth, then it is so. If you harness this energy to manifest the house of your dreams or the perfect relationship, then it will soon be yours.

But it's important to understand that this is only the first step and is by no means the actual goal. Every time you *get* the thing you focus on, your ego is satisfied momentarily. The problem is that the ego can never get enough. Once a goal has been achieved, you become aware of the fact that the inner longing, which prompted the initial inquiry, is still there and hasn't been satisfied at all. So you move on to the following item on the list—the next thing or condition that you believe will finally fulfill this deep, unfathomable well. Time after time this process is repeated until you finally come to a profound realization: there's nothing in the *outside* world that can satisfy the longing you feel.

It's time for a new strategy . . . it's time to look *within*.

You're now ready to move on to the second level of the Moses Code, what I referred to earlier as the Body (representing the soul). You've realized that the ego can never be satisfied by anything in the outside world and that true satisfaction only comes from imitating the qualities and patterns of God. This requires a new decision, one that leads in a different direction. Let's focus our attention to the soul.

Let's return to the analogy I used earlier—where the light cast against a body created a shadow on the ground that was then mistaken for reality. We've shifted our gaze away from the shadow and back to the thing that created it: the body. If the shadow is a representation of the ego, then the body becomes a symbol of the soul. Once we realize the futility of trying to fulfill the ego's desires, we begin shifting our attention in this direction.

Imagine that your back is toward the light so that you're looking at the shadow. It's now time to turn around and face the light once again, symbolically disregarding the desires of the ego. Turning to the light is the equivalent of choosing to *see as God sees,* seeking the gifts of the soul over those that will never satisfy you.

You may wonder, *What does it mean to see as God sees?* In every moment of your life, you can choose how you perceive what's around you—that is, the people in your life, the circumstances you experience, and the events you encounter. If you decide to see through the eyes of the ego (the Shadow), you'll see everything as separate and isolated. As I've said before, one of the beliefs of the ego is that you must defend yourself from what's outside and may attack you without warning. You observe the world through suspicious eyes, unable to truly perceive except through a darkened filter. The people or circumstances that could have served you well or brought you great joy are disregarded or even attacked—all because you chose to see the world in this way.

If you choose to see through the eyes of the soul, then the world and everything in it appears in a very different light. You realize that you aren't separate from anything or anyone but are intimately linked with the reality you observe. There's no need to attack because you know that you'd only be attacking yourself. The only thing left to do is to bless everything you perceive, because in the end, every experience is guiding you into a deeper understanding of your highest purpose in life.

Earlier, you read that the ego seeks to *get* while the soul seeks to *give.* This is because the soul—now facing the light as opposed to facing the shadow—seeks to imitate the light, or God. The soul is really the link or bridge between the ego and the Divine. Once you've crossed that bridge and merged your consciousness with God, its purpose is complete and it identifies itself as one with its Creator. In other words, the soul is absorbed back into the intention of God, extending and expanding exactly as God extends and expands. The two have become one, and only oneness exists.

This leads us to the final stage—the Light.

This is the source of everything you perceive, which illuminates and creates the Body (soul) and the Shadow (ego). The goal of the Moses Code is to shift from identifying yourself with the ego to seeing through the eyes of the soul, and then finally remembering that in reality you're neither of these. You are the Light—one with the Source that shines upon the rest of creation. This is your aim, but achieving it will require more of you than you can possibly imagine at this time.

At the beginning of Part II, you were given the opportunity to stop and enjoy the lessons you've learned, using them to attract everything you've ever desired into your life. If you chose to stop there, you would have possessed the necessary tools to manifest whatever reality you wished, and for a moment, you would have been appeased. But that satisfaction wouldn't have lasted long because you would have only achieved the desires of the ego and wouldn't have realized that there's a deeper longing—your soul, which can never be appeased with any physical accomplishment. The soul seeks something that lies beyond this world, something that can't be defined or removed by time or death. It searches for the eternal —or at least qualities of the everlasting—which does manifest in this world.

What are some of these qualities?

- Peace
- Love
- Grace
- Joy
- Patience

These are present both here and in Heaven, which is defined as a state of consciousness rather than a place you enter when you die. They're like solid bridges connecting this world to the real one—a world based upon the laws of Oneness rather than of separation. The ego and the soul are like vehicles that carry us into these various dimensions but only as far as they're able to go. For example, if you were driving a car and reached the beach, you wouldn't be able to drive any farther. You'd need a boat to carry you to the other side of the ocean. But if you didn't have the time it would take to travel by boat, then you'd need a jet to get you there faster.

The ego is like the car. It can carry you on land, but it's very limited when it comes to other needs. The boat can ferry you over water, but even it is limited and can only get you to the other side over a long period of time. Only the jet can transport you to any place you need to go, because it's able to rise above the earth and isn't bound by the terrain. It doesn't matter if you're traveling through a desert or over a mountain. Its ability to ascend to a higher altitude enables it to overcome the restrictions of the world below.

In the first part of this book, you were driving a car and the ego was in charge of everything. Then you moved to a boat, and the soul began to take you to the places that the car couldn't reach. Now it's time to board a jet, for where you're going can't be accessed by the car or the boat. This jet will rise above the earth and take you into a new realm, one that isn't bound by the laws or customs of the past.

From here, you move into the Light.

Exercise #10:
Claiming Oneness

You're going to use the Moses Code to see through the eyes of the soul, which is the same as *seeing as God sees*. As often as you can today, look around and observe the people around you as if they are a part of you. You already know that this is true—that you're one with everything and everyone. This will give you the chance to practically apply this in your life, and in doing so, you'll feel this reality through your whole being.

Whenever you find yourself in an area where there are people moving about, breathe out, saying, "I AM THAT." Try to identify with a particular person as you say this, and do your best to *feel* that it's true. In other words, don't simply recite the words—let your emotions fill the empty spaces that seem to exist between you and the other person.

Then breathe in, and say, "I AM," knowing that you're claiming this oneness with the individual as God. It's one thing to say that you're one with God, but your goal here is to literally feel this reality, thereby *knowing* that it's true. In doing so, the statement is no longer a simple concept, but an experience that can be loved and shared.

CHAPTER ELEVEN

EGO VS. SOUL

Up to this point, we've been using an analogy to help describe the sacred journey of the Code—the Shadow, the Body, and the Light. Now we'll return to the story of Moses in order to gain deeper insight.

There are actually three figures in the drama when the turning point occurs—the instant when the Holy Name is given to Moses and, ultimately, to the whole world. If you recall, Moses was tending his sheep when he saw a bush that was on fire without being consumed. He then heard a voice speak to him, giving him the mission of securing the freedom of the Israelites.

The name of God, I AM THAT I AM, possesses the force that Moses will need to create miracles, demonstrating the fact that true power doesn't come from earthly riches but from the realization of our oneness with God.

Now we'll apply the Moses story to our original analogy:

1. The Shadow (ego) now becomes Moses.

2. The Body (soul) now becomes the burning bush.

3. The Light continues to represent God/ the Voice.

The primary quality of the ego is that it seeks outside itself everything it believes will satisfy its longing. Moses believed that the Hebrews could never be happy until they were free, and freedom, of course, meant being released from Egyptian bondage. But "outer" liberty without the consciousness of genuine freedom does very little to relieve the deeper desire. That's why the Israelites were unable to leave behind the symbol of slavery, an idol they created in the form of a golden calf. The influence of their Egyptian captors still ruled their minds, and when push came to shove, they abandoned their monotheistic roots in favor of polytheism.

This would be an interesting exercise for all of us—what are the golden calves we hold on to just in case things don't work out the way we hope? The Israelites neglected the inner work that would bring the freedom they sought, and when they found themselves alone in the desert, they pulled out the symbol of bondage—the golden calf—as if it could save them. What are symbols of limitations you cling to and are afraid to let go of? Maybe it's the security of a special relationship or a certain amount of money in your bank account. Be willing to release your grip on these things and trust that beyond all these symbols your soul is leading you to the promised land.

The foundation of polytheism is that there are many gods, all of whom are separate from each other and humanity. Such a concept is in full conformity with the demands and expectations of the ego, since it's completely unable to comprehend singularity. Moses, however, went to the Israelites and the Pharaoh with a different agenda. He came to show the Pharaoh that *God is one,* and it must have been an enormous disappointment for the king when his own people began abandoning the polytheistic foundation.

THE EGO'S AGENDA

The ego has only one agenda: its own survival. Because it's ultimately an illusion, the ego must use everything at its disposal to continue the false images it creates. That's why it's so quick to abandon one belief in favor of another even though the two may oppose each other. Even when the ego has plenty of evidence to support the truth—in this case, the fact that Moses was able to secure the release of the Hebrews using the power inherent in the name of God—the moment this evidence doesn't serve its agenda, it's disregarded. It would rather flip-flop than die, for death is its greatest fear. The ego convinces you that if it dies, you die, so you become a willing conspirator in this farce. This is how the ego rationalizes every decision it makes, making it seem quite reasonable to follow one path this moment, then the opposite the next.

Moses (and the Israelites) represents the part of all of us that would rather trust the evidence of separation rather than the promises of the Divine. God promised that the Hebrews would be led to a "land overflowing with milk and honey," the land of their birthright. But the moment the desert winds began to blow, they questioned their ability to survive and went back to their comfort zone—a decision that ultimately deprived them of this great reward.

Simply put, the ego's power is insignificant; therefore, it must seek it everywhere else in order to receive more. Unfortunately, most people in this world live within this limited belief. They believe that they can do very little on their own, much like how Moses felt at the beginning of his journey. Anything that is weak must be bolstered by something that's strong, so the ego chooses to seek its strength *outside* in order to make itself feel more powerful.

The soul, on the other hand, realizes that there's nothing outside that can help it in any way. Genuine strength lies within, and when we operate from the wisdom contained within our soul, we feel empowered to create in a new way. When we live from the soul, we quickly realize that the true function of life is to create and extend as God creates and extends. Then the powerlessness of the ego is overcome, and we achieve a level of satisfaction that the mind can never comprehend.

The soul accomplishes this, as I've said before, by giving what it desires. If peace is the goal, then the soul offers peace to others. If love is the intention, it's expressed everywhere and to everyone. The soul immediately receives these gifts because it realizes that it isn't separate from the soul of another person. In other words, there's ultimately one soul expressing itself in an infinite number of ways. Through service, we move from the limiting beliefs of the ego into the expansiveness of the soul. Finally, as the soul remembers its oneness with every other soul, we move into the Light—that is, God. Complete and Divine abundance is achieved.

From this point on in our study, we'll apply Moses's conversation with God as the framework for understanding the Code and using it to attract everything we could ever desire. Once again, Moses represents the ego, the part of us that perceives Divine abundance as something existing outside of ourselves; the burning bush represents the soul, the part of us that burns away the ego's desires and seeks a higher vision and call; and God is the true goal, the most supreme part of us that remembers its one-ness with all reality. The Moses Code is ultimately the fusion of these aspects, drawing upon each of them to create peace in our lives and in the world.

The question before you now is simple: Who are you in this drama of manifestation? Are you Moses, using the techniques you've learned to attract all the things you don't currently possess, believing they'll enrich your life? Are you the burning bush, ablaze with the energy of creation and offering it to everyone you encounter? Or are you God, aware of the intimate connection you share with every living being and fully present with the heart of Divinity itself?

The choice has always been yours, and your awareness is based on the figure you choose to embody. The fact that you've come this far indicates that you've finally realized the futility of the ego's path. You may have successfully attracted all the things you thought would satisfy your inner longing —houses, cars, and abundance—but the yearning never really left no matter how much *stuff* you accumulated. You may have even learned the art of giving what your soul most desires, and in doing so, you've realized that it was always yours. Yet there is still a final step to take, one that your mind can't truly comprehend.

CHAPTER TWELVE

THE FINAL STEP

Is it time to step into that reality now? Are you ready to finally attain the true and highest goal of the Moses Code? If so, you'll reunite your awareness with the awareness of God and realize that you are One with your Creator. Don't be surprised if this makes you quake a bit, filling your heart with both excitement and panic. It's only natural, but as you've read over and over, the ending is sure. You wouldn't be reading this if you weren't ready or if you hadn't called this into your life. All you need to do is step forward. The angels will do the rest.

Imagine that you've been playing a role in a dramatic play for so many years that the thin line separating the character you've created and the real you has become blurred. Instead of taking off the costume and makeup when the performance is over, you return home and pretend that you're still the character. Whenever circumstances arise that require your attention or response, you decide to act according to this fictitious person who doesn't really exist. In doing so, the truth in you has become obscured, and you've lost track of your genuine needs and desires. The *you* who God perceives has fallen asleep, and it seems that you may never be awake again.

But your awakening was preordained, and if you choose to, you can remember and wake up from the dream of separation today—this very moment. You were fooled into believing that it takes time and that you'd have to *change* who you are in order to *be* who you really are. Does that make any sense at all? Why would you have to change to become your authentic self? Now the insanity of the ego is made clear, and it's time to set it aside forever in favor of the vision of God that never changes.

Let's read that once again: the vision of God that never changes. Even while you played a role from a play you wrote on your own, God has never forgotten who you really are. And if God hasn't forgotten, neither have you. This is the greatest news in the Universe because it signifies that you've been protected from all the meaningless concepts you've created to hide from who you really are. They've never existed at all except in your own imagination. What other choice do you have now but to rouse yourself, stretch, and realize that you've never actually left your true home? You were protected and safe from the beginning, and there was nothing you ever did—no sin committed or error embraced—that changed anything at all.

If you are one with God and God hasn't forgotten who you really are, then it should be easy for you to wake up and remember. What changes when you finally accomplish this?

Nothing at all.

Once again, only your ego believes that you must change—that everything about you and around you transforms when you finally accept the truth.

Many of us have ideas of how we might act when we become "enlightened." The main one is probably this—you'll be different than how you are now. There's a line in *A Course in Miracles* I love: "Enlightenment is but a recognition, not a change at all." In other words, when you finally open your spiritual eyes, you will See what has always been Seen by God. All the shadows that seem to obscure your Real Self will vanish, and you'll realize that you are filled with Light. Isn't this what it means to be enlightened? The truth is, you're filled and overflowing with Light right now, if only you could recognize that fact. Let this be the moment!

Have you ever imagined how you might act when you're finally enlightened? Does it include imitating someone you perceive to be different from you, someone you believe to be awake? In other words, when you wake up, maybe you'll behave more like that person than yourself. If the individual is from another country, believes in a different religion, and speaks with an unfamiliar accent, the ego is very happy because then it has every reason to deny who you are right now. It looks out at all the illusions you create about what it means to be enlightened and says, "Someday you may be like that."

But someday never comes.

The idea that you must alter who you are in order to be enlightened is one of the ego's main defenses against the truth—regardless of whether or not the illusion is working for you, you're more afraid of change than you are of realizing the truth. You fear what it might mean to possess such power and how you might act when you're so free. However, these are fears that aren't based on anything that's real; they're only the shadows of reality. What is real can't be threatened or threatening. Accept this and it is so, for this is what the journey of awakening is all about.

So how does all this apply to the Moses Code? Simply put, the final step in this process—recognizing that you're one with God and, therefore, have been called to act as God in the world—is the most threatening thing in the Universe. It's easy to accept that you must give up the ego's insistence on *getting* everything you believe to be outside yourself. It's even easy for you to realize that giving and receiving are the same. But the idea that you are actually one with God . . . this, you can't fully embrace. In fact, you'll do anything and everything to avoid accepting this on the deepest level.

So what's the answer? How do you release all the hidden and primordial fears that have kept you from realizing the truth?

You don't!

Wait a minute. Maybe this is something new, something unforeseen that you've never imagined before. You may wonder, Don't do anything at all? Don't even try to release the final illusion of separation—the very thing that has kept me from realizing that I'm already enlightened?

Do you feel yourself relaxing with the understanding that you don't need to do anything at all? That's the whole idea. When you're afraid of something, you build walls of protection that are difficult or even impossible for you to overcome. But when you're at ease, the walls are very low to the ground— so low that any child could cross them. The goal is to help you stop putting pressure on yourself to *do* anything at all . . .

. . . but to allow it to be done for you.

Let's take a breath for a moment. All this time you've been focused on what you need to do to practice the Moses Code in order to attract everything you really desire. Then you've shifted the focus of this, giving to others what you desire, but at least it was easy to tell who was doing the work. You were, but now you're being told something very different. You're being asked to step back and do nothing at all, and in doing nothing, everything will happen on its own.

Not exactly.

What you're actually being asked to do is hold still, once and for all, and let God take the final step for you. You've already done everything you need to do. You've stepped beyond the ego's endless desires and have adopted a new way of looking at the world and everything in it. You've also learned how to give what you most desire, thereby realizing that it has been within you all along. You've done an amazing job and should be commended for it.

But this final step isn't yours to take; the sooner you discover this, the quicker it will happen. It's literally a step away from this world into eternity. Until now, the decisions you've made have been predicated on your belief in time, space, and all the limitations therein. It's time to trust the One who doesn't know these limitations—the One who has the sacred role of removing you from all the things time would claim, establishing your heart in the real world.

In other words, you can't take this final step on your own, but it can be taken for you. This is the step that God must take, for only then will you realize that you and God are one.

Here's the best part. The step I'm describing was actually taken a very long time ago, before time began—that is, it's a step that leads nowhere except where you've always been. It's the step that leads to your heart and to the Heaven that has always been your home.

This is a journey without distance. Our only goal has been to realize—not in our minds but within our hearts—that the truth in us has never changed, and we have the ability and the right to live within that truth now . . . this very moment. There's nothing we need to do and nothing we need to alter, for what we're now focused on can never change, no matter what happens. This may be one of the hardest things for any of us to accept, because until now we've been told the opposite. We've been taught that we have the ability to lose our Divine Inheritance through sin or making choices that destroy the soul.

What we're learning now is that there's nothing in this world that can destroy the soul, since God's love is unconditional. We may be able to delay our awareness of this love, but it's inevitable.

Now you have the opportunity to accept the final step in the Moses Code, embracing your eternal oneness with your Divine Source. Is it hard for you to acknowledge that this solution has always been so close—that it was nothing more than a choice away? However, that isn't the question you should be asking yourself, since the past is gone and means nothing. The only appropriate question is, Will you embrace it now?

How will you answer?

If you say yes, then God will take the step you've been unable to take yourself, and you'll remember who you are. Gone are the days of striving after the ego's endless appetite. All that you're left with are the open rewards of Heaven, here and now, waiting for you to receive and share. This is what God does, and now it's yours to do the same.

The Moses Code is now complete within you. Your decision was all that was needed and then your willingness to step back and allow God to take the final step. The world and everything in it now fades and dissolves into this Holy Purpose, for it is your purpose as well.

Take a deep breath and allow it to be true.

FINAL THOUGHTS FOR PART II

Welcome home. You began this journey focused on everything that you perceived to be outside—all the things you thought you needed to be happy and fulfilled. Then you realized that there was nothing outside of the truth within you, and you began offering that gift to everyone in order to realize and remember it for yourself. Finally, you chose to be still and allow the last step to be taken for you, the step away from the world you created and into the world created by God.

The journey is now complete, but not because I say it is. You'll experience the true fulfillment of your highest desire when you claim it, and this can only come from you. There will always be those who remind you of what you already know, but the willingness to step into the light is yours alone. The Moses Code is a gift from Heaven, a conversation that leads you into the Divine relationship that fulfills every hope and dream you could ever conceive. There's nothing outside the *you* God created—nothing for you to receive from anyone or anything that isn't already fully present within. Embrace it and it is yours, for the truth will never abandon you.

Moses may have never reached the promised land, but you have. You did it by realizing that there's nowhere for you to go at all; you discovered where you've always been: Heaven. There's no desert to cross, no Pharaoh to battle . . . there's nothing but your own thoughts and the decisions you make about yourself. Claim to be One with God and speak with the voice for God, and everything else is given to you automatically. The Kingdom of Heaven is all around you this very moment. Open your eyes and see, and only then will you be truly seen.

AFTERWORD

Nothing is impossible unless you say it is. What do you say is unachievable? Did you believe that it was impossible for you to realize your heart's longing and be satisfied on every level of your life? Did you decide that there are some things you deserve and others you don't, or that you're only worthy of a small share of the Kingdom of God?

If there's one thing you take from this book, I hope it is this: you deserve the *whole* Kingdom, not just a portion of it. And how will you realize this? By simply giving it to others. Your soul wants to give just as God gives. Your ego wants you to hold back because this is what it does—it holds everything back from you. The only question to ask yourself is: *Who is offering me more?* Has the ego's path ever given you what you've wanted, or have its empty promises finally forced you to look in a new direction? Now your gaze is focused toward Heaven, for you realize that the gifts of God are the only things that will bring you happiness and peace. And here's the best news of all:

The gifts of God are already yours!

You don't need to deserve them, nor do you have to change who you are to receive them. All you have to do is say yes, and they'll flow toward you from every direction. This is why you were born, and it's the reason why you picked up this book. Heaven is opening before you and offering the gifts you really desire. There's nothing left for you to do but open your heart and allow these blessings to extend to everyone you meet. It's the only way to ensure that the flow never ends.

So say *yes*, and get on with the great task that lies before you now. Heaven's gates have been opened wide, and it's time for you to enter with an open and grateful heart.

THE DEEP END OF THE POOL

You now have all the information you need to activate the most powerful manifestation tool in the history of the world. It's time to enter into the full *experience* of the Moses Code. Understanding this spiritual tool is just the first step. Realizing the full potential of your soul by allowing a fundamental shift to take place can happen only if you're willing to take one final leap. Your intellectual understanding of this sacred technology is important, but without the actual experience, it will fade and drift away. Our goal isn't to just understand the Code, but to literally *become* it!

I couldn't have written this final chapter when this book was first published, but now that I've had over a decade to teach and learn this technology, I'm ready to swim in the deep end of the pool and invite you to join me there. We're about to step beyond intellectual information and enter the experience your soul is longing for. This is the essence of the Moses Code, the full embodiment of your I AM Consciousness.

What do I mean when I say I AM Consciousness? It might be easier to understand it if I break consciousness into two parts: the split mind or ego-consciousness, and the whole mind or I AM Consciousness.

It's easy for us to understand the split or dualistic mind, since it's the primary way we see everything— separate from who we believe ourselves to be. The ego claims, "I am this, but I am *not* that," thus creating an entire world where we challenge and compete with every other separate part. I AM Consciousness is very different. It acknowledges only one reality and sees everything contained within that oneness. It says, "I AM this AND I AM that." Do you see the difference? Actually, let me put that another way: Do you *feel* the difference?

It's common for people to ask, "Do you believe in God?" When we're getting to know someone, we might be curious about their spiritual heritage or religious upbringing. I have a new answer when people ask me that question. I say, "No, I don't believe in a God." Of course, they're usually shocked, considering that I've written many books and given literally thousands of talks on the matter. I usually let my answer sink in a bit before finishing the thought. "It's true, I don't believe in a God—what I believe in is *only* God." They usually give me a confused look until they understand what I'm really saying. "God is *all* there is."

Do I know this intellectually? Of course not. Such an experience is beyond the intellect. But I *know* it nonetheless.

Like me, you were probably raised to think of God in a very different light, some of which we've already discussed in this book. God is "out there," far beyond our experience. We may even think of God as having human or emotional attributes, quick to anger if we don't do everything we're told to do, everything our religions tell us are holy or just. I remember when my friend Reverend Michael Beckwith said: "God made us in his image and likeness and we tried to return the favor." In other words, our image of God says a lot more about us than it does about God. We're quick to anger and attack, so God must be the same.

No! Stop right there. This is the first step for entering into the actual experience of the Code. God is nothing like your split judgmental mind. God doesn't think like your ego-mind. God is Wholeness Itself! When I say I don't believe in a God, I believe in *only* God, I mean that quite literally. God is everything and everywhere, omniscient and omnipresent. In his book *The Universal Christ*, Father Richard Rohr describes the Christ in a very similar way: "The Christ is just another word for everything."

But here's the problem we face: Our ego-based split mind is incapable of understanding everything. Only our whole mind can understand something that is beyond our conceptual mind-set. Instead of using our dualistic mind, we must return to our original way of seeing everything—through our non-dual mind.

Bonus Exercise: A New Way of Seeing

Here's a little exercise that will show you what I mean. It will only take about 10 seconds, but it will give you a clear example of the difference between dualistic vision and non-dual vision. The whole point is to realize that what we think we see is not necessarily what's really there.

You've likely heard it said, or even experienced yourself, that the world is really an illusion or part of a great dream, albeit one that's very convincing. But when you think about it, doesn't the same thing apply to your nighttime dreams as well? When you're dreaming, everything you see is very convincing and you don't question its reality. If someone hits your arm you say, "Ouch," or if someone tells a joke, you laugh. You don't look at the person and say, "I would laugh if that was a real joke, but since neither of us are really here, it's not funny at all." You believe what you see and have faith in what you feel, and it's only when you wake up in the morning that you look back at the dream and realize none of it was real.

Is it such a leap to believe that something similar might be happening right now? You may respond by saying, "Yes, but there's consistency in my waking state. I go to sleep and wake up in the same bed, and I have memories from my childhood and everything else that has ever happened to me." You'd be correct in this. It's true that consistency seems to prove that what's happening right now is real and not a dream, but here's where it gets interesting:

You said the same thing last night when you were asleep and dreaming.

I don't mean this literally, but imagine someone saying the same thing to you in your dream state. "This is just a dream, you know . . . there's absolutely nothing that's consistent." You would look at them and say, "What are you talking about? I fell asleep and woke up in the same bed and have vivid memories of my childhood. How can you say I'm dreaming?"

Do you see what just happened here? When you're asleep and dreaming at night, it seems like everything happening to you is consistent and real. You believe that you have memories of childhood, or your wedding, or anything else . . . but do you? All those memories are manufactured to convince you that you're experiencing consistent patterns and that you have a past you can verify. But the moment you wake up in the morning, you sit up in your bed and say, "None of that was real, and there was no consistency at all."

The *exact* same thing happens when you wake up from this dream. You will sit up and for a moment think about the things you saw or experienced and say, "None of that was real!"

And now for the exercise. Remember, the point of this is to demonstrate that what you see isn't necessarily real. All it takes is a slight shift in focus and you see something completely different.

Hold your hand in front of your face and hold out one finger. Focus on that finger. You can see what's there—one finger. It's obvious and clear, right? Now shift your focus and look at something in the distance. If you're outside, look at a tree or a cloud, and if you're inside, focus on a picture on the wall. Make sure the object is a good distance away, not right in front of you, and make sure you're looking through your finger.

In other words, don't look to the left or right of your finger. Look through it. How does your finger change when you look at something in the distance? What do you see?

Two fingers!

But you know very well that there's only one finger to see, and as soon as you shift your focus back to your hand, *two* shifts back into *one*. And this, quite simply, is the real goal of using the Code—to allow *two* to shift back to *one*.

THE EXPERIENCE OF ONE

Using the above exercise, it's easy to see how a tiny shift in focus can make us see something that isn't really there. You might think that was a poor illustration because it was so simple, and perhaps you'd be right. On the other hand, the simplest examples are usually the clearest and help us see something that's been in front of us all along. I could write chapters and even books on why we choose to perceive an illusory world over the world that can be seen by our soul, but words won't help us at this point. What we really need is an experience that's so direct and compelling it will be impossible to deny. What's required is a direct encounter with the single truth this book, and the 3,500-year-old code, have been trying to get us to see.

Let me share a story from my own life.

I've spent many years traveling to war zones and areas of conflict to perform a peace concert made up of the peace prayers from the 12 major religions of the world, the first being Croatia and Bosnia in 1995. When I was in Croatia, I heard about a group of mystics who lived in the mountains along the Croatian-Bosnian border. They were called the Emissaries of Light, and from what I was told, they had existed in one place or another for hundreds or even thousands of years. At first, I thought they were playing a trick on me, but the story continued. The friends I met were meant to bring me to visit the community, something that was usually never allowed. This was the reason I was invited to the region. They had a message to deliver to the world, and for some reason they had chosen me to deliver it.

You need to know that at this time I had no platform (a term that wouldn't even be used for another 15 years or so, when social media and e-mail became the primary means of communicating). I also had no idea how I would share a message of such global importance. If what they were saying was true, these mystics had been meditating for peace 12 hours a day in areas of war and conflict, extending what they called Divine Light to neutralize the violence and hatred in the world. It sounded too fantastic, but the adventurer in me had to see for myself.

What followed became the subject of my first book, *Emissary of Light*, published in 1996. I was led into the forest with several other people, where we finally met 13 men and women who lived in complete secrecy and usually in complete silence. They would leave their tiny cabins every night at midnight and meet in a dome-shaped building where a 12-spoked wheel was painted on the floor. They would sit around that wheel until noon, then would stand and silently walk back to their cabins.

As interesting as that was, it was not the reason I was there. I would sit against the wall every night while the Emissaries meditated, and I wondered if it was possible for me to sit still for 12 hours. Looking back, it's still hard to imagine how time passed so quickly. It felt like no more than an hour or two had passed before a chime sounded and the 13 Emissaries stood up and left the room. It was only then that I noticed the sun was shining bright and 12 hours had passed.

An hour or so after the 12-hour meditation, I was summoned each day to the cabin of the one I called Teacher, an elderly man who sat in the center of the wheel while the other 12 sat cross-legged at each of the outer spokes. These meetings remain one of the highlights of my life and initiated what I've referred to as the "Experience." It wouldn't have been possible to discover the Moses Code if it wasn't for those afternoon chats, so informal yet powerful beyond measure. My teacher's influence seemed to open something inside me, a door I thought was locked, but with a bit of musical insight, opened like magic.

He called it the Door of Eternity, and so now I'll share exactly what he said to me:

"You must step through the Door of Eternity, the door that leads away from time. This is the step that all other lessons have led to. It begins with the release of fear, then sees past the illusion of separation. Once you've allowed Divine Light to build within you and permeate your being, only then are you ready to see the Door. All it takes is a shift in perception to see it" (*Emissary of Light*).

Once again, a simple shift in perception, like seeing one finger instead of two. This entire book, *The Moses Code*, is meant to prepare you for that simple shift, but the final step is one you must take alone. It began with learning how to use the Code to manifest what you think you need to feel happy or fulfilled. Then we shifted gears and began focusing on manifesting goodness rather than just goods. Every exercise led a little deeper toward the final step—stepping into the actual experience, or as Teacher said, stepping through the Door of Eternity.

Are you ready to take that step?

When I was with the Emissaries, Teacher said that he wanted me to share a simple message with the world, and for the next decade or so I was completely dedicated to sharing it word for word. He said:

"Just tell people the truth, that they're ready for this."

I remember the look on most people's faces when I shared this. "You are ready!" It was as if I was giving them permission to relax and stop trying to *get* ready. Most of us think we'll be ready after we've read enough books or attended more workshops. But the truth is, you're ready *right now*, and that's the only lesson the Emissaries were here to teach. And I think it's the final lesson of this book as well.

You might be asking yourself: "Ready for what?" Let me see if I can answer that question, even though it's very difficult to put into words. I could say you're ready to leave your limiting beliefs and step into a new level of awakened or I AM Consciousness. Or I could say that you're ready to be happy all the time, even when you're not. That may sound funny, but it's something I say all the time—*I'm happy even when I'm not*. What I mean is that no matter what happens on the outside, my inner experience is set at a level of such peace and gratitude that I'm able to deal with anything that happens with grace and ease. I'm not shaken or disturbed by changing forms, but am completely secure within that which never changes and yet is always in motion. That's what you're ready for, if you choose to accept the challenge.

And it is a challenge. You may hear or read the words, but you have to say *yes* before they're activated within you. Most of us, instead of saying yes, say something like "I'll be ready soon" or "Give me a few more years, and I'll have everything in order." Don't you realize that that day never comes? You'll never have everything in order, simply because this is a world of disorder. The world you see around you is meant to keep you distracted from this realization, the realization that you're never going to have everything in place or perfectly organized. There will always be more—another project or another job. The challenge is to say *yes* even when things do seem undone or incomplete. Just say, "*Yes, I am ready!*" and let the chips fall where they may. You may find that for the first time in your life, they fall perfectly into place.

I wrote earlier that what we all need is an experience that's so direct and compelling that it would be hard to deny. Like shifting your focus from seeing two fingers to seeing only one, it's time for you to leave the world of the split or dual mind and finally accept your I AM Consciousness. If you've read this far, then you must have accepted that there's something of value here. You must feel something beginning to dissolve and something else beginning to awaken. It's time for you to make a choice, one that may make all the difference for you.

Are you ready to finally accept that love is the very essence of who you are, and that there's nothing you need to do to deserve that experience?

Say *yes!* Say it out loud. Really mean it. It really is that simple. In fact, lay this book down right now and stand in front of a mirror, look yourself in the eyes, and say: "*I AM Love, I AM.*" Say it several times and let the energy seep into your soul, then when you're ready say: "*I AM Perfect, I AM.*" Once again, take a deep breath and let that feeling take hold. Then, when you're ready, say these words with more conviction than you've ever had before: "*I AM Awake, I AM.*"

What do you feel when you say these words? I'm confident that you'll feel something moving inside you, similar to when you first open your eyes in the morning, stretch, and begin the day. You're waking up through the power of the name of God that was given to Moses 3,500 years ago. I promise that what you're feeling is real, and if you continue with this and every other practice from this book, you'll realize that for yourself.

My advice is to nurture that energy just as you would a tiny baby. If you were holding a baby in your arms right now, you would take care of it and make sure it has what it needs to grow, until the day when it can finally stand on its own. Jesus once said that if your child asked you for a fish, you wouldn't give them a rock instead. God has given you one of the greatest gifts in the history of the world—the Sacred Name— EHYEH ASHER EHYEH—I AM THAT, I AM. If you say *yes* to being ready for it, the Name will take root in you and you'll begin to see everyone you meet, yourself included, as God sees them—perfect, holy, and complete. If you say *yes* to being ready, the world itself will begin to change around you, and you'll realize for yourself that things here aren't as solid and consistent as you thought. If you say *yes*, and really mean it, the experience I've been describing will take over your life in ways you can't even begin to imagine.

And now I'll leave you to discover all this on your own. All I can say is that it's been a true gift rediscovering this amazing sacred technology we call the Moses Code and reintroducing it to the world. I believe millions more will discover its power and activate it in their lives. And when they do . . . well, of this we cannot speak.

James Twyman
August 2020

APPENDIX

A SHORT COURSE
IN MANIFESTATION

The subtitle of this book is "The Most Powerful Manifestation Tool in the History of the World." At first that may have seemed like a grand claim, or it may have even been the very thing that determined whether or not you picked up the book. I'd like to add that I truly believe that the Moses Code is the most powerful technique I've ever encountered. Why? Because I've experienced firsthand the transformative power of combining the name of God with other traditional manifestation practices. However, I'm not asserting that other practices don't have their place, and that's why I'm adding this section to the book. For the Moses Code to be most effective, it's important to understand some of the fundamental elements for creating everything you desire.

In 2006, millions of people around the world became excited about a documentary called *The Secret,* which described on a basic level a phenomenon called the Law of Attraction. I was very excited when I saw the film, and I even added some of the techniques to my own practice. However, I was also a bit worried by two aspects of *The Secret.* First of all, it seemed to be almost completely focused on using the Law of Attraction to *get* the things that would hopefully add happiness or contentment to your life. If you don't like your car, you can use it to get a better one. If you don't like your house, you can manifest one that fulfills your wildest dreams. It all sounds good, but there were some very important elements, or deeper secrets, that seemed to have been left out.

The other thing that worried me about the film was that I felt it oversimplified the process of manifestation, leaving out critical ingredients that could determine a person's success or failure. I began hearing about many people who followed the techniques and practices, believing that everything in their lives would suddenly shift. For some it did, but for many it didn't. Unfortunately, some of those who failed decided to throw out the entire process and simply give up. They concluded that there wasn't a secret at all and returned to their lives of victimhood.

One day I was discussing all of this with my friend Debbie Ford, the author of many best-selling books, including *The Dark Side of the Light Chasers.* She, like many other spiritual teachers I know, had very strong feelings on the subject and wanted to find a way to offer a more complete version of the

Law of Attraction and show how we can use it to fulfill our lives. We decided to ask a few of our friends to join us in a series of conference calls that would explore using the art of manifestation to *give* rather than simply *get*. I'm a strong proponent of viewing acts of service as a powerful path to enlightenment, and I know for certain that trying to satisfy the endless needs of the ego leads to complete disillusionment. Unfortunately, this is what my colleagues and I are seeing over and over with people who are practicing the *Secret*.

The conference calls were referred to as *Using the Secret to Create Peace.* Along with Neale Donald Walsch, Michael Beckwith, Jean Houston, and James Ray, Debbie and I launched the course. I wasn't at all surprised when more than 13,000 people from around the world signed up, listening and participating in this vital conversation. It seemed that there were more people than we imagined who were ready to take the next step.

Even though I'm being honest with my feelings regarding the focus of *The Secret,* I also want to say that I believe it was a critically important step for many of the individuals who watched it. Realizing that we create everything we experience—no matter how positive or negative it may seem—is the first step in spiritual mastery. But it's only the beginning, and we shouldn't think that we're in graduate school when we're really in first grade. It became increasingly clear that we needed another, more comprehensive look at the Law of Attraction.

A week after the conference calls were completed, Debbie contacted me and related an interesting idea. She asked if I'd be willing to work with her on a new film, one that would help people who felt disenfranchised by *The Secret*. She didn't know that months earlier I'd decided to get out of the movie business, having been overwhelmed by the energy it took to produce or direct three other films, including *Indigo*, a feature about spiritually open children. Lucky for me, she was persistent and finally convinced me that humanity needed another look at this subject.

We considered several angles and explored working with other successful filmmakers, but in the end I felt that the Moses Code offered everything I wanted to express. I was already well into writing this book and decided to combine my efforts for a one-two punch: a powerful written work that would be supported by a convincing film.

My goal with both of these projects has been to share my experience with the Moses Code while also offering a solid foundation in the significant elements of manifestation practices. When these are combined, they create a potent energy that's more powerful than anything I've witnessed before. The next section in this Appendix will be focused on these techniques—the framework that's essential in making the Law of Attraction work. Use what makes sense and feel free to disregard what doesn't. In the end you're the authority, and your willingness to activate your connection with your own Sacred Self is the only thing you need to be successful.

Most of the people who try to implement the Law of Attraction and fail are unaware of the issues that are blocking their ability to manifest their desires. This is usually because they haven't done the work required to clearly attract what they think they want. The reason I say "think they want" is because contrary to their belief, the technique is actually working perfectly.

Human beings are complex, and unfortunately, one-dimensional solutions rarely solve intricate problems. Most of the manifestation techniques and tools that are popular today are valuable and can produce wonderful benefits, but only if a proper foundation is laid that allows them to have the greatest effect. Making a list of affirmations and reciting them over and over is a powerful tool, but saying *I am an abundant being* to yourself does very little if deep down—beneath your conscious mind—you believe the opposite.

There are many worthwhile programs that can help you appropriately and effectively address these issues, so I won't attempt to include them here. However, one that I can strongly recommend is the Shadow Process, a retreat offered by Debbie Ford. I attended Debbie's workshop and can honestly say that it changed my life, giving me tools to deal with the shadows that blocked my ability to attract what I really want in life.

For now, I simply want to add that this work is essential if you want to truly attract goodness and blessings into your life. As powerful as the Moses Code is, you have within you the power of God, and it can't be taken away. Your wish is the Universe's command, whether it's conscious or unconscious. It will give you everything you ask for, so it's vital that you know exactly *what it is* you're asking for. Otherwise, you'll practice these techniques and pull into your life all the things you believe you don't want, and you'll say that it doesn't work. It does work—every time!

Now it's time for you to do the work so that your soul's desire—not your ego's—will be realized.

THE 10 KEYS
TO MANIFESTING
EVERYTHING
YOU DESIRE

1. Be clear.
2. Be open.
3. Be willing.
4. Be happy.
5. Be focused.

6. Be expectant.
7. Be energetic.
8. Be positive.
9. Be true.
10. Be grateful.

These are some of the most important keys to help you manifest everything you want to attract into your life. You'll notice that each one starts with the word *be*—for example, *Be clear.* That's because they're focused less on what you need to do and more on what you need to be.

"You must be the change you wish to see in the world."

— GANDHI

How many times have we talked about all the things we believe or want, but deep down we were unwilling to integrate the qualities that would attract them? Words mean very little if our lives don't reflect what we say. St. Francis of Assisi once said: "Preach the Gospel always, and if necessary, use words." That is, the words we use are secondary to the way we live our lives.

Have you ever met people who said all the right things, but when you were with them, something didn't feel quite right? It's as if there's a radar detector within us that feels what our mind alone can't sense. On the other hand, have you ever been with those who said very little, but you find yourself inexplicably happy when you're in their presence? These are the ones who have perfected the *art of being,* the essential ingredient to attracting everything you could ever desire.

These ten keys are guidelines, and there are others you may add as well. They aren't in any particular order, since everyone will have a different experience according to their own personal makeup. Read them and find ways to integrate them into your own life. Most of all, don't try to analyze them with your logical mind as much as live them in the ordinary moments of your life.

We often expect our lives to be determined by extraordinary experiences when it's usually the everyday situations that teach us the most.

1. Be Clear.

You've probably heard the saying, "Be careful what you ask for, because you just might get it." Have you ever been in a situation where you thought you wanted something—really wanted it—and then put all your energy into achieving that goal, only to find out that it wasn't what you wanted at all? You may have also experienced the inability to focus enough on a specific goal and ended up attracting something that didn't fully align with the original intention.

Clarity is one of the most important keys to manifesting what you want. If your thoughts aren't clear, then the Universe—that is, God—doesn't know how or what to give you. If there's something you've already determined for yourself (remember that you should never try to create something for another person), write a list of every detail you can think of, every attribute and characteristic that defines the goal. Look at this list often and add to it. Focus on the details as clearly as you can and imagine them in your mind. God loves clear thoughts, while the ego loves what is confused and muddled.

Clarity also means simplicity. The simpler you make the details, the straighter the shot will be. Try not to overcomplicate your goal, but allow it to reveal itself to you in as straightforward a manner as possible. If it's clear to you, it will also be clear to God, and the path to achieving your desire will be unencumbered.

2. Be Open.

Your mind is like a parachute—it works best when it's open. It's hard to argue with that logic. A closed mind is no use to anyone because it believes it already knows the path to walk and may therefore miss new opportunities when they present themselves. The ability to remain open when your mind or heart is fixed on a particular object or outcome may be a tricky proposition, but it's essential in attracting the energy required for manifesting your dreams.

Being clear and open may initially seem like opposing concepts. In the first case, you were asked to clearly define exactly what you're determined to manifest. Now you're being asked to be open to new movements—anything the Universe may send in your direction that either amplifies or clarifies the desired goal. In reality, they are supportive, one following the other. Once you've clearly defined the desired experience and have set your mind to a particular form, you then open yourself to every possible variation. It's as if you declare to the Universe: "This or more."

Being open is the same as surrendering, an experience that is foreign to the ego but is completely comfortable for the soul. To the ego, surrendering is the same as failure; to the soul, it's the first step toward ultimate victory. It shows God that you're willing to trust a higher vision—one that you'll be ready to embrace at any given moment. In this way, openness and clarity go together, like two siblings who may be different but can't live without each other.

3. Be Willing.

Your willingness to observe, absorb, and then release everything that comes into your consciousness will help determine how easily it flows into your life. Begin by observing what you desire:

- Is it something that will serve more than your own self-interests—that is, would it benefit humanity and the whole world as well? If it's something that fills your cup alone, then it isn't worthy because it won't teach you the higher lesson that every gift you offer to another was already within you.

- Is it something that you can absorb into your heart as well as your mind? It's important that you're able to *feel* the gift you're about to receive, for your mind alone can't contain the higher goals that you truly desire. In other words, don't sell yourself short. A new car is a wonderful gift and something you can certainly manifest and appreciate, but does it genuinely inspire your heart? Would it inspire the hearts of others? You're capable of absorbing so much, so go for it.

- Are you able to release or surrender the goal, then trust that it will flow to you naturally and easily? If not, you may find yourself forcing what was never intended to be yours. Try to resist the urge for your ego to lead the way, and allow God to give you everything that already belongs to you.

4. Be Happy.

This is a key that can't be overemphasized. As you've read, God's will for you is perfect joy. *Perfect joy!* This means there's a degree of happiness that neither the world nor the ego can understand but your heart is constantly striving to achieve. This is what you truly desire, for it's the joy that bridges Heaven and Earth. By accepting this, you also become a symbol to others who are as worthy of this gift as you are. When you realize that you deserve perfect joy and accept it, you become the kind of teacher the world needs most. You're an example of the only thing that fulfills each one of us.

Does happiness seem like a small thing to you? The truth is that we often sacrifice it in order to receive the gifts our ego desires, neglecting the simpler things that serve us on deeper and more essential levels. This is usually linked to how we're perceived by others in the world. Feeding a person who is in need might satisfy you more than eating in the fanciest restaurant. Helping someone who is homeless might fill you with more joy than adding a new addition to your own home. Your soul doesn't seek what pumps up your feelings of self-worth. It's happy only when you give this gift to others—then your self-worth is expanded in ways that the mind can never comprehend.

5. Be Focused.

Stay focused on what's behind the goal rather than on the goal itself. Ask yourself, *Why am I seeking this gift in the first place? What's the motivating desire that I'm not looking at?* Perhaps you're concentrating on attracting a new home. What's the motivating desire or need that's inspiring you to create this? Maybe you don't feel safe where you're living now, or you don't feel abundant in your house. Focus for a moment on that, really feel it, and then ask yourself where it's coming from. Once you discover the answer, focus on fulfilling what lies deeper in your heart. This will allow the perfect home to appear on its own. It may not be the one you first envisioned— it may be simpler or smaller than your first choice— but you'll be satisfied with it in a way you wouldn't have been with one that was larger or more grandiose. This is because you tuned in to your inner self and fulfilled the deeper desire of your soul.

We usually think of focus as something that's fixed and straight. I suggest thinking of it as fluid and flowing. When you realize that your mind doesn't always know what's best for you and that a strict, unyielding mind-set might attract something that doesn't serve your highest good, then opening to a flowing focus starts to make sense. Trust that your heart knows more than your mind when it comes to these things, and let a more gentle focus guide your path.

6. Be Expectant.

Always expect the best! Affirm that everything you desire will come to you easily and naturally. Remember that energy flows where attention goes. If you're focused on creating something, but your inner thoughts are fixed on failure, that's what you'll attract. Energy, like water, always seeks the deepest well or spring and naturally flows in its direction. Try to become aware of your deeper thoughts and impulses, and if needed, extend some love in their direction. Focusing love usually means that you're open, understanding, and uncritical. You'll discover that you'll be able to soothe your doubts better with love rather than criticism. Negative attention only serves to reinforce the patterns that created the block, whereas loving-kindness dissolves everything in its path.

We've all heard the saying, "Expect a miracle." This is very good advice, because what you truly expect will always be yours. The trick is to uncover the impulses that determine what you're really asking for, not just what's most obvious. Then you'll be able to proceed with a clear mind and open heart, and whatever you ask for will be yours. That's one of the most crucial lessons to learn in the art of attraction: God always gives you what you ask for. So stop asking for what you *don't* want, and expect what you *do*. This is the sign of true mastery.

7. Be Energetic.

The higher the impulse, the more energetic the response. In other words, your energy usually increases when you ask for what your soul really wants. For example, imagine that your attention is focused on manifesting a new car. Some people are extremely passionate about automobiles, but most simply follow the current trends or opinions. Does the desire for a new car align with what your soul desires? What might inspire you more? Perhaps you've always wanted to travel but never had the chance, or you've wanted to pick up a particular skill or new hobby but haven't had the confidence to do that either. Planning an around-the-world cruise would create more positive energy than a car, as would deciding to take art lessons. Let your passion be your guide, and the energy required will follow.

Being energetic is also contagious. If you're speaking to friends and are describing something that you're trying to attract into your life, but they don't feel any passion behind your focus, then they won't be able to help you by adding more energy. However, if they feel inspired by your vision, two things will probably happen. First, they'll fuel your enthusiasm by adding more energy to yours. Second, they'll be positively influenced by your energy and will go out and create something for themselves—something that inspires their lives. The key is to follow your heart, not your mind. Your heart is always a better barometer of what Heaven is choosing to add to your life.

8. Be Positive.

This key is an absolute. If you're negative about what you're trying to attract, the Universe will interpret your negativity as *not wanting*, and you won't achieve your goal.

The problem is that this energy can sometimes be hard to discern. It hides in your consciousness and evades the obvious movements of your rational mind. That's because the blocks to your positivity are often nonrational, even though they wear the clothes of the most optimistic person you've ever met. Remember that every thought or goal has a sponsoring thought—and there are also sponsoring thoughts to your sponsoring thoughts. (Is it starting to sound complicated?) The point is that your surface thoughts may not represent what's happening beneath the surface, but energy will still flow to the more powerful force.

The key isn't to overcomplicate the issue and believe that you must unearth layer after layer of beliefs that have ruled your life. Simply be willing to look and then bless. Sometimes these negative beliefs just need you to acknowledge them, and then they can move on their way. As long as you're conscious of them, they can be addressed quickly and effectively. Then you'll be able to move on to the next step.

9. Be True.

This key follows from where the last one left off. Being true is the same as being honest—something that's required if you want to successfully manifest your heart's desire. Remember that the Universe always seeks to give you what you really want. But if you're confused about what you desire, the Universe will be unsure about what to give you. Most of these lessons are focused on helping you be clear—then to clearly manifest.

Many people think that all they need to do is follow a simple list of instructions, and everything will directly flow to them. In theory this is accurate, but most individuals haven't done the inner work that's required in order to allow the process to be successful. They run through the directions they've been given and it doesn't work. Some then decide that they aren't like others who are able to attract good things, believing they don't have the ability to achieve their desires. This is unfortunate, as it's a gift that each one of us possesses to the same degree simply because we were all created by the same God. The only difference is that some people have completed their inner work and others haven't. Being true means being true to yourself, and this is a gift that no one can give you but . . . guess who?

You have to be honest with yourself. There's no substitute for this, and no one can be honest for you. You can practice all the keys to manifestation that you're being offered here, but if you're not willing to be true, you'll only succeed in attracting what doesn't serve your highest good. Notice that I didn't say that you'd be bound to fail, because failure is impossible. The question to ask yourself is: *How do I succeed in attracting what my soul wants?*

The answer is to always do the work that's required to sweep away the limiting beliefs that have been blocking you. Then everything you truly want will flow naturally in your direction, all because you were honest with yourself and willing to look closely at the hidden desires that you weren't able to see before.

10. Be Grateful.

Gratitude is perhaps the most important key to attracting everything you deserve. It's the activating force that God can't deny, and the Universe bows to a heart filled with Divine appreciation. And you are no different. When someone is grateful for a gift you've offered or a small act of kindness you've shown, it makes you want to give even more. On the other hand, if you offer a gift to someone and the receiver is ungrateful, you may be offended. At the very least, you'll be less likely to give again because you feel that the gift won't be fully appreciated.

The Universe works in a similar way, so be grateful for every gift from God, no matter how big or small. God doesn't understand the difference between small gifts and large ones—they're all the same because they come from the same heart. In addition, be grateful for your failures as well as your successes. We tend to learn more from the ways we don't succeed than we do from success itself. Once the lesson has been learned, you can move forward and avoid making the same mistake again, all because you were grateful in a way that completely transcends logic.

THE 10 BLOCKS
TO MANIFESTING
EVERYTHING
YOU DESIRE

1. Not worthy
2. Not ready
3. Not clear
4. Not enthusiastic
5. Not open
6. Not healthy
7. Not willing
8. Not prepared
9. Not helpful
10. Not realistic

1. Not Worthy

Everyone in the world at one time or another has felt unworthy of attracting goodness into their lives. Perhaps a difficult childhood or other traumatic experiences have led us to adopt these limiting or devastating beliefs about ourselves. We sometimes assume that these thoughts are laid out in concrete and we'll never be able to move past them. However, the opposite is true.

You have the opportunity to be reborn and have the fresh start you've been denying yourself. The first step is to know that it's possible and then to step into that possibility. Are you ready? If you say yes, a brand-new world awaits you right now.

You are worthy of every gift you desire for one reason: *You're a perfect child of God in this and every moment.* Reading this book means that you have at least some belief in the Universal Power we sometimes call God. It doesn't really matter how you practice, but the knowledge that there's a force beyond your own limited abilities is vital in releasing the patterns that have controlled you until now.

I believe that God sees each one of us as whole and perfect regardless of what we've done in the past or what we'll do in the future. In other words, God loves us for who we are right now. If this is true, none of the terrible things you've done in the past mean anything. They're simply the experiences that brought you to this moment, and it's here that you can accept a new vision—the one held by God that allows you to attract into your life everything that is good and worthy of a perfect child of God. Then you'll be able to see yourself exactly as God sees you and know that you're worthy of every gift you've previously denied yourself.

2. Not Ready

In the previous section, I asked if you believe that you're ready to accept the gifts you deserve. I'm hoping you said yes, for your admission of this fact is the beginning of your final acceptance of everything that's already yours. So what does that mean exactly?

As I've explained many times, the gifts you truly want are the ones that are already within you, not outside of you. The ego seeks to *get* the things it perceives as outside itself in order to secure a longer life, while your spirit—or your soul—seeks to *give* the things you really want, thereby realizing that they were already there within you.

What are these gifts? Perhaps one we can all agree on is love, as we're all seeking to experience it in every area of our lives. We want to be loved by our children, our partner, our friends, and even people we barely know. We desire this because we ultimately want to believe that we're lovable—that is, worthy of being loved.

Therefore, most of the things your ego seeks are designed to make you seem more lovable. Why? Because the ego has a very different vision of you than God does. God perceives you to be completely deserving of love no matter what you think, say, or do. Your ego, on the other hand, rarely accepts this. Even when you prove yourself to be loving, it doubts that it will last. Around the corner, there surely lies evidence that proves you don't deserve to be loved. So your ego conjures up an elaborate charade that attempts to show others that its negative vision of you isn't true. It begins gathering *things* around you that it believes will help you fool others. If you have the right car, an elaborate house, or anything else it designs, then you'll be worthy of the attention of someone far more wonderful than you.

God doesn't believe anything like this. There's nothing you can accumulate around you that can alter the truth. God sees you as holy, and the only thing that is worthy of one so holy is love itself. Therefore, God spreads love before your every step, but its effect is lost unless you're willing to claim it for yourself. You're challenged to trust one voice or the other.

Jesus said, "No one can serve two masters" (Mt 6:24). You also can't trust two different voices, especially when they completely contradict one another. You are either holy or vile. Which will you choose? If you choose holiness and are deserving of love, you'll be asked to offer that gift to someone else. Then you'll be able to claim it for yourself. It's only when you act as God in the world—giving to others what they deserve—will you discover that the gifts you truly want have always been within you. They were hidden, yes, and even forgotten, but they never left you. Through this act of service, you discover the truth of who you are, and in doing so, you realize that you're ready for anything.

3. Not Clear

One of the things that may block you from realizing your heart's intent is that you're not clear about what you're really asking for. As I wrote before, you may be clear about what you *think* you're requesting, but if something else is appearing in your life, then there's an issue you're not consciously aware of.

You already know that God gives you everything you ask for. If you want to know what you really want, simply look at what's showing up in your life. It's the perfect arbitrator, since it never lies. If you think you're asking for the perfect relationship, but you consistently attract people who don't appreciate you, take you for granted, or never listen to what you feel is important, then what you're actually asking for is someone who doesn't appreciate you, takes you for granted, and doesn't listen!

Okay, let's start there. Even this can be a beginning for attracting what will serve your soul. Let's take the judgment out of the equation and simply *be clear* about what's really happening. In your mind, you're asking for the perfect partner, but what keeps showing up is someone who's as imperfect as you. Ah, maybe there's a clue here. If everything you perceive is really a reflection of the decisions you're making about yourself, then it's your opinion about you that needs to change—not your opinion of the other person.

Now we're getting a clearer picture. As I've said, inner work is usually required to undo the limiting beliefs that have previously held you back. The question is: Do you want to continue to see yourself in this light, or are you willing to begin anew? Why not begin focusing on the things about you that you really love? Since everything you focus on increases, this may be the perfect exercise. Get a vivid picture of the parts of yourself that you really want to attract instead of the parts you don't. It begins with clarity, but it will end with your receiving what your soul has been longing for.

4. Not Enthusiastic

One of the keys to attracting what you really want is to be energetic about your desires. The more energy you give something, the more it will give back to you. Enthusiasm is very similar to this and should be viewed in the same light.

If you aren't enthusiastic about what you're creating, the Universe won't take you seriously. For example, if you meet someone you're attracted to and are interested in asking this person out for a date, it's customary to show some enthusiasm. It gives the other person the signal that you think he or she is special, and your energy alone may be enough to get a date.

But what happens if you show no eagerness at all? You ask the person out with little emotion and in a monotone voice, and this individual will probably look at you and think you're kidding, assuming that there must be some other agenda, because you clearly aren't interested in going on a real date.

When you approach the Universe in this way, you achieve the same results. It's important to get excited about what you're asking for, since it's a form of energy. We've already established that giving and receiving are the same thing, and the more energy you give, the more you'll receive. You can't expect to get something you don't give, so don't expect God to give you something you're not really committed to. Enthusiasm is a form of commitment, so be selective and only focus on what you're really passionate about.

5. Not Open

It's impossible to walk through a door that isn't open. Likewise, it's impossible for you to receive anything if *you* aren't open. Some of the blocks I'm sharing may seem completely obvious, yet these are the ones that are commonly missed. Just because something is out in the open doesn't mean that we see it. We may also view it with our mind but not perceive it with our heart—in other words, we don't really understand it and won't be open to receiving it.

Don't be fooled into thinking that you already know all of this—or worse still, that you're immune to these blocks. Over the years, I've learned that I'm immune to nothing. I fall into the same traps as everyone else, and it helps to remind me that I still have some growing to do.

Just because you've learned something, it doesn't mean the lesson is over. Think about this: the only real journey you ever take is a journey of 13 inches—from the mind to the heart. I can't tell you how many times I've studied a lesson in my mind but then failed to practice it in a real situation. I've also caught myself forgetting something I already learned without even realizing that I was doing it. It's important to acknowledge that you're always growing and getting better. Be open to seeing your challenges as well as your victories. This is the surest way to continue evolving, attracting what you truly desire with greater expertise.

6. Not Healthy

The following question is simple, and it's vital that you answer it as clearly and honestly as possible: *Does the goal you seek create harmony or discord?*

This is essentially what health is: balance and harmony. If the goal you're focusing on sets you off balance and doesn't promote your well-being on every level, then I suggest you either release it or allow it to shift to something new—something that promotes good health in every way. You certainly have the power within you to create whatever you choose—what blesses and heals you as well as what brings division and discord into your life.

Remember, though, that whatever you offer to others and the world you also offer to yourself. You may even use the Moses Code to hurt another person, but be very careful. Through this process, you've trod close to Heaven, and it's important that this altar remains clear of anything other than the highest intent. Act as God would and use the power contained in the Code to promote well-being and healing for everyone you encounter, and then it will surely be yours.

7. Not Willing

If you're not willing to work toward the goal you seek, then it may be best to let it go and save yourself the trouble. This isn't meant for those who wish to wave a magic wand or recite a secret formula that takes responsibility away from them. In most cases, this process requires a fundamental shift in those who are manifesting a new reality for themselves. Being willing to do the inner work shows that you're ready to receive—and not to just wish and wait for action. There's an enormous difference between the two, and your determination must demonstrate it in order to prove that you're worthy of the gift.

Willingness shows the Universe that you're flexible and able to constantly challenge yourself, looking at everything from various angles and perspectives. If you lock yourself into one direction or path, you may miss new possibilities that God presents. Don't forget that when you enter this stream of creation, you are, in essence, becoming a co-creator with the Divine. God is manifesting with and as you, and you would do well to align yourself with this power, recognizing Divine inspiration when it's offered to you.

Be willing to acknowledge that you may not see the whole picture right now, and that your focus, though intense, should also be open to new possibilities. At first this may seem like an admission of weakness, but it's really a sign of wisdom and strength. If you aren't willing to adapt and grow, you'll continue to manifest realities that reflect your inflexibility. However, if you approach this process with humility and grace, it will open up for you like a Divine flower, spreading its fragrance into your life in ways you can't imagine.

8. Not Prepared

When I was a Boy Scout, I was told to always be prepared. It was our motto, and it also applies in the world of manifestation. It's important for you to be prepared to actually receive the gifts you've focused on. It shows the Universe that you're serious and willing to lay the groundwork for accomplishing the goal. If you want to concentrate on manifesting a new home, begin by finding a real-estate agent who can help you. If you're focused on attracting a partner who will bring love and energy into your life, then find other ways to generate those things in your life. As I've already stated, energy attracts more energy, so don't be afraid to prime the pump.

Take the necessary steps to make sure that you're truly prepared. If the goal that you're seeking is nothing more than a fantasy, bring it into the realm of reality. If you wish to attract the perfect mate but there's no room in your life to welcome that person, create some space as soon as possible! If you want to manifest a new home but can't get approval for a loan, repair your credit rating. Then you'll be ready when the perfect house comes along.

Being prepared means holding the space open for a new reality to come streaming in. If you're unprepared, it won't matter if the goal is staring you right in the face. You won't be ready, and it will disappear as quickly as it came.

9. Not Helpful

Here's a great idea: if you wish to learn the art of manifestation, help others learn it first. Sometimes the best way to understand something is to teach it. This definitely applies to me, and it probably rings true for you too. I've spent my life teaching the principles of peacemaking because it's what I want to learn most. I discovered that the more I teach it, the more I comprehend it. It may seem like a backward approach, but I know from experience that it works.

One of my friends decided to teach a class on abundance at a local church. I was surprised, because in my mind this person was anything but abundant. For instance, he was in the process of losing his house and had to borrow money to get by. I felt some judgment and even considered saying something, perhaps suggesting that he begin practicing how to achieve abundance before trying to teach the principles to others.

But then something amazing happened. Weeks after the class began, my friend's financial situation started to transform. A source of funding for a project opened up that he'd been working on for several years, and his business improved at the same time. In short, the more my friend helped others achieve abundance, the more it flowed toward him. It's one of the best examples I've ever seen of how giving and receiving are the same.

10. Not Realistic

This final element that blocks what you're trying to achieve is difficult to explain. You've heard over and over that you're capable of attracting everything you set your mind to—and it's true. But there's also an element of reality that must be worked into the equation. For example, if you're focusing all your will on becoming an all-star NBA player but you're 40 years old and out of shape, you may want to take a look at what you really want. This isn't meant to limit your creation in any way; rather, it's to recognize when your real motivation is to *seek but not find.*

Unfortunately, we sometimes set goals that we'll never achieve in order to prove that we don't really deserve them. Our ego wants to look back and say, "See, I told you this wouldn't work! Now go back to where you belong."

Be aware of this when you set your goals. It's something that most people deal with, so don't be surprised if it comes up for you too. If you decide what you'd like to manifest, ask yourself: *Is this what I really want, or is there something else that will satisfy my soul?* If you set the goal of manifesting a house that costs $3 million, but you're currently earning $50,000 a year, take a look at your motivation. If you're really serious, begin by taking steps to reach the place where you can afford a multimillion-dollar home. As I wrote earlier, nothing is impossible unless you say it is. The key is to become aware of what you're saying.

A NOTE FROM
THE AUTHOR

Several months ago, I was asked to lecture at a sound-healing conference in San Francisco. One of my good friends, Jonathan Goldman, was also speaking there, and while we were having lunch, I explained the details of the Moses Code to him. Then I asked Jonathan if he knew of any sounds or frequencies that were associated with the Sacred Name of God as given to Moses. He said that he'd be happy to do some research and would discuss his findings with me. What follows is a detailed account of Jonathan's revolutionary discoveries as he experimented with tuning forks that directly corresponded to the name of God. As you read about his work, you'll be as amazed and fascinated as I was.

I believe that Jonathan's research proves that the mysteries behind the Code go far deeper than we first imagined. The fact that the Holy Names of God are actually encoded in these frequencies proves that we're indeed living in a multidimensional Universe, and the reality of God pervades every level.

THE I AM THAT I AM FREQUENCIES

by Jonathan Goldman

Our ancient mystics and quantum physicists are in agreement: everything is sound. From the electrons moving around the nucleus of an atom to planets in distant galaxies orbiting their suns, everything is in a state of vibration. This includes the chair you may be sitting on or the pages of this book you're reading. Our bodies are also complex compositions of vibration.

If you examine the basic tenets of the various religious belief systems on Earth, you'll find a commonality in their understanding that the initial creative force—what scientists call the big bang—was indeed sound. This creative force has been referred to as "the Word" by St. John. The Old Testament tells us, "In the beginning, the Lord said: 'Let there be Light!'" The actual act of speaking created the energy of light; thus, sound preceded light.

Sound travels as waves—known as its "frequency" —and they're measured in cycles per second (scientifically written as hertz, abbreviated as Hz). Slow sound waves manifest very deep sounds; fast sound waves create high ones. We're able to pick up from around 16 to 20,000 Hz. That's our spectrum of hearing. Nevertheless, creatures such as dolphins can receive and project frequencies upward of 180,000 Hz—about ten times our level of hearing! As the ancient mystics have told us: "Everything is sound." We need to understand that sound encompasses much more than our limited range of hearing.

THE MANY NAMES OF GOD

One of my focuses of using sound as a healing and sacred modality is what's known as "the Sacred or Holy Names." These are the various names of God found in many different traditions. In particular, I've worked with the Sacred Name in the Hindu and Tibetan traditions, where there are numerous deities with different attributes. I've also investigated the sounding of the Sacred Name of God in the Jewish and Christian traditions utilizing traditional biblical texts, as well as lost books of the Bible and kabbalistic sources.

One of my projects involving the name of God is called *The Divine Name*. (It's available from Hay House as a CD, co-created with my friend and colleague Gregg Braden, the author of *The Divine Matrix* and *The God Code*.) The concept of the *Divine Name* first manifested through a dream I had many years ago. It was a sounding of the tetragrammaton—that is, the four-letter name of God found in the Old Testament as YHWH—created completely through vowel sounds. When I sounded these specific vowel sounds, it was among the most powerful tones I'd ever experienced. Because of its energy, it took more than ten years before Gregg and I released this discovery to the public. (For those who are interested in reading more about this, there's a tremendous amount of information in the liner notes accompanying the CD.)

GEMATRIA

One of my areas of interest is gematria, which is an ancient system from the kabbalistic tradition in which specific numbers are assigned to letters of the Hebrew alphabet. Numbers can, in turn, be assigned to whole words, phrases, or more. Gematria is a mystical type of numerology that has powerful applications. Numerous books are available on the subject; in particular, I've often used *Godwin's Cabalistic Encyclopedia,* by David Godwin, to assist me with this work.

During my initial meeting with James Twyman at a sound healing conference, we both wondered if there were any special numbers associated with the phrase "EHYEH ASHER EHYEH." These were the words that the Divine Being spoke to Moses on Mount Sinai when he asked for the Divine's name. The reply, pronounced as "EHYEH ASHER EHYEH," is often translated as "I AM THAT I AM."

When I returned home from the conference, I remembered my discussion with James and immediately began consulting kabbalistic sources to see if there were any numerical references to this Holy Name. I was delighted and surprised to find that indeed there were. "EHYEH" had the numerical value of 21, "ASHER" had the numerical value of 501, and the entire phrase had the value of 543 (21+501+21).

Please understand that while I work with sound—which is numerically measured in cycles per second called frequencies—I'd never personally encountered a specific relationship between the numeric value of a name and the frequency of this name. I'd tried this previously to no avail.

However, something strange and unique occurred that night as I went over the gematria for the Holy Name.

I'm frequently directed by inner guidance. That was true this night as I stared at the different numbers. I knew that what I was looking for wasn't merely a single number, such as 543, but two numerals. In addition, I was looking for these two numbers to be close enough to each other so that they were within the same range of an octave.

OCTAVES

An octave is a musical term. It's either the tone above a given frequency with twice as many vibrations per second (Hz) as the original, or it's the tone below a given frequency with half as many vibrations (Hz) as the original. For example, if one frequency is 100 Hz, the octave above this frequency would be 200 Hz. If you wanted to find the octave above that, 200 Hz, you would simply double that figure again, which would result in an octave at 400 Hz. Conversely, if you wished to find the lower octave of 400 Hz, you'd simply halve it and come up with 200 Hz. When this number is halved again, it would be 100 Hz, creating the octave below 200

Hz. The concept of the octave is easy to understand; however, it may have profound implications.

Regarding the law of octaves, there's an ancient hermetic principle: "As above, so below." Frequently in the world of sound healing, people are often doubling or halving a frequency to see if they can create a correspondence with something else.

The reason why I was looking for two numbers rather than one—specifically, two numbers that fell within the same octave—is that my experiences have recently demonstrated that there's more power in the vibrations of two objects simultaneously vibrating than there is in one simple vibration. When there are two vibrations, they can create a specific field if they're in a particular kind of relationship with each other—that is, within the range of an octave. Many think the fields that are generated have specific powers and abilities, and some assert that they may even be likened to a kind of interdimensional portal.

I've done a tremendous amount of work with regard to the power of the relationship of two different notes. Most often, I do this by creating tuning forks with the two notes, and then experiencing the results of their effects by listening to them. Sometimes these sounds can be quite extraordinary. More than a dozen years ago, I discovered several powerful healing sonic relationships, including being the first to acknowledge the importance of the ratio of 8 to 13 and then developing tuning forks cut to this ratio. The response to these tuning forks has been overwhelming, and now, more than ten years later, an entire line of "phi"-based ratio tuning forks are being marketed.

Thus, after my initial conversation with James, I was wondering if it might be possible to have tuning forks made in order to create frequencies that utilized numbers from the gematria of I AM THAT I AM. I would not, however, know what this musical interval would sound like until the tuning forks could be created and experienced.

In truth, in my research with sound, I've experimented with numerous varieties of numbers by listening to the frequencies produced by their corresponding tuning forks. Sometimes these numbers can be powerful and healing. When two different tuning forks are sounded together, the results can be wonderful. Other times, however, they create extremely unpleasant tones. Also, their effects can be the opposite of healing, but you can never know that until you hear them firsthand.

Before the tuning forks could be created, I had to decide on the frequencies that would be used. Because I'd wanted to create tuning forks within the same octave, I used mathematics to see if I could get both numbers within the same range. Sensing that 501 (the numerical value of "ASHER") would make an excellent frequency for one tuning fork, I also began working with the number 21, the numerical equivalent for the Holy Name "EHYEH."

Then I started doubling it: 21 - 42 - 84 - 168 - 336 - 672. I looked at the number 672 and intuitively knew that there was something significant about it. I looked up the gematria of this number in the *Cabalistic Encyclopedia* to see if there was any special meaning contained in it. There was! For example, 168 was the numerical equivalent of the words *to protect.* I continued looking up numbers. Then I stopped in seeming disbelief as I discovered that 672 was the equivalent of another Holy Name—the name YHVH ELOHIM. The number was also translated as "to receive illumination." The hair stood up on the back of my neck—there was something very powerful in this number!

I then had tuning forks cut for 168 Hz, 336 Hz, and 672 Hz to represent the sound of the "EHYEH." Likewise, I had tuning forks cut to the 501 Hz and to lower octaves of this: 250.5 Hz and 125.25 Hz.

My next step was to wait until I received the tuning forks so I could begin experimentation. When I'm guided to have tuning forks cut to specific frequencies, I never know what the results will sound like, but I'm always open to the possibility that the forks I've had created might not sound pleasant.

I was really excited when the I AM THAT I AM tuning forks arrived. I gently tapped them together and listened to their powerful yet soothing frequencies. I was so excited! As I listened to the sound, I was given the intuitive knowledge that the tone was creating a field of Divine Energy—I call it the I AM THAT I AM field. All the different octaves of the I AM THAT I AM tuning forks produced tranquil and sacred sounds, creating a field of light and love. In addition, I created a recording containing all these different octaves that seemed to possess a synergistic, extraordinary effect of all these sounds.

For those with a musical inclination, the frequencies of the I AM THAT I AM field come close to creating the interval (the musical relationship) of the 4th—with the first note somewhere between a B and a C, and the second note somewhere between an E and an F. This interval of the 4th has been studied and researched by various sonic practitioners, as some hold that it balances the nervous system, increases the auric field, and may even expand our consciousness. There are many other positive attributes associated with this interval. Its use in Gregorian chant is of particular note. The odds that these two numbers created via gematria and octaves should manifest a positive sonic relationship such as this are probably astronomical, as is the mathematical association between the "EHYEH" and "YHVH ELOHIM" numbers.

In my books, including *The 7 Secrets of Sound Healing* (Hay House), I present a formula I created: "Frequency + Intent = Healing." "Frequency," as discussed in the beginning of this writing, is the actual sound being created—the cycles per second of the sound. "Intent" is the energy behind this sound—the consciousness that is encoded on the sound. "Intent" is important to both the person creating the sound as well as the person receiving the sound. "Healing" in this formula represents the desired outcome of the sound. Depending upon the person and their intent, other aspects of consciousness could be substituted for the word *Healing,* including concepts such as "Peace" and "Harmony." Perhaps the specific frequencies of these I AM THAT I AM tuning forks, when combined with a particular intent of those experiencing these sounds, are indeed an extraordinary tool for healing, manifestation, and spiritual activation.

After my experiments, I can only speculate upon these tuning forks possessing an extraordinary relationship that's positive and beneficial to those who receive their energies. Reports from people have indicated amazing healing and sacred responses from those experiencing the I AM THAT I AM field. As I stated, their sound together is both beautiful and soothing. In addition, people who have listened to them have indicated that they hold amazing healing properties and help initiate and enhance sacred experiences.

The I AM THAT I AM tuning forks and the associated field created by them is a provocative and exciting sound experience, and the potential is promising, particularly with regard to assisting the I AM THAT I AM breathing exercises that James has developed for *The Moses Code.* I'm most grateful to be a part of this powerful new sonic discovery.

Jonathan Goldman is an international authority on sound healing and a pioneer in the field of harmonics. He is the author of *Healing Sounds; Shifting Frequencies; The Lost Chord; Chakra Frequencies: Tantra of Sound* (co-authored with his wife, Andi Goldman), which won the 2006 Visionary Award for Best Alternative Health Book; and his latest, *The 7 Secrets of Sound Healing.* Jonathan presents Healing Sounds Seminars throughout the world. He is the director of the Sound Healers Association and president of Spirit Music, Inc., in Boulder, Colorado. A Grammy nominee, Jonathan has created numerous best-selling, award-winning recordings, including *The Divine Name* (with Gregg Braden); *Reiki Chants; Ultimate Om; The Lost Chord;* and *Chakra Chants,* winner of the Visionary Award for Best Healing-Meditation Album. He is also a lecturing member of the International Society for Music and Medicine.

To learn more about Jonathan's work, please visit: www.healingsounds.com or www.soundhealers association.org.

ABOUT THE AUTHOR

James F. Twyman is the bestselling author of 16 books, including *The Barn Dance* and *Giovanni and the Camino of St. Francis.* He's also an internationally renowned 'Peace Troubadour' who has the reputation for drawing millions of people together in prayer to positively influence crises throughout the world. He has been invited by leaders of countries such as Iraq, Northern Ireland, South Africa, Bosnia, Croatia and Serbia to perform the Peace Concert – often while conflicts raged in those areas; and he has performed at the United Nations, the Pentagon and more. James is also the executive producer and co-writer of the feature film *Indigo,* and the director of the documentary *The Moses Code* as well as five other feature films including the award-winning *Redwood Highway.* James currently lives at Namaste Lake Chapala, a spiritual community he founded in Ajijic, Mexico, and is a Franciscan Friar in the Community of Francis and Clare. **www.JamesFTwyman.com**

Bonus Content

With the book, you have free access to the *I AM Wishes Fulfilled Meditation* audio download, featuring an introduction from Dr. Wayne W. Dyer and the Moses Code meditation. The Divine sounds in this meditation were reproduced from the exact sounds associated with the name of God, translated from Hebrew as I AM THAT, I AM, using tuning forks. These sounds, accompanied by your personal I AM mantra, offer you the chance to manifest your desires and live a wishes fulfilled life.

Visit https://www.hayhouse.com/downloads and enter the Product ID 2746 and Download Code audio.

Hay House Titles of Related Interest

YOU CAN HEAL YOUR LIFE, the movie,
starring Louise Hay & Friends
(available as a 1-DVD programme, an expanded 2-DVD set
and an online streaming video)
Learn more at www.hayhouse.com/louise-movie

THE SHIFT, the movie, starring Dr Wayne W. Dyer
(available as a 1-DVD programme, an expanded 2-DVD set
and an online streaming video)
Learn more at www.hayhouse.com/the-shift-movie

———✦———

*THE COURSE IN MIRACLES EXPERIMENT: A Starter Kit for
Rewiring Your Mind (and Therefore the World),* by Pam Grout

*HAPPINESS IS THE WAY: How to Reframe Your Thinking and Work
with What You Already Have to Live the Life of Your Dreams,*
by Dr Wayne W. Dyer

*THE POWER OF AWAKENING: Mindfulness Practices and Spiritual
Tools to Transform Your Life,* by Dr Wayne W. Dyer

*THANK & GROW RICH: A 30-Day Experiment in Shameless
Gratitude and Unabashed Joy,* by Pam Grout

THE UNIVERSE HAS YOUR BACK: Transform Fear to Faith,
by Gabrielle Bernstein

All of the above are available at www.hayhouse.co.uk

———✦———

HAY HOUSE

Look within

Join the conversation about latest products,
events, exclusive offers and more.

 Hay House

 @HayHouseUK

 @hayhouseuk

 healyourlife.com

We'd love to hear from you!